Microsoft® Office
PowerPoint® 2007
Top 100

Simplified®

TIPS & TRICKS

by Paul McFedries

Visual™

Wiley Publishing, Inc.

Microsoft® Office PowerPoint® 2007: Top 100 Simplified® Tips & Tricks

Published by
Wiley Publishing, Inc.
111 River Street
Hoboken, NJ 07030-5774

Published simultaneously in Canada

Copyright © 2007 by Wiley Publishing, Inc.,
Indianapolis, Indiana

ISBN: 978-0-470-13196-1

Manufactured in the United States of America

10 9 8 7 6 5 4 3 2 1

Trademark Acknowledgments

Contact Us

For general information on our other products and services contact our Customer Care Department within the U.S. at 800-762-2974, outside the U.S. at 317-572-3993 or fax 317-572-4002.

For technical support please visit www.wiley.com/techsupport.

WILEY

Wiley Publishing, Inc.

U.S. Sales

Contact Wiley at (800) 762-2974 or fax (317) 572-4002.

PRAISE FOR VISUAL BOOKS

"I have to praise you and your company on the fine products you turn out. I have twelve Visual books in my house. They were instrumental in helping me pass a difficult computer course. Thank you for creating books that are easy to follow. Keep turning out those quality books."

Gordon Justin (Brielle, NJ)

"What fantastic teaching books you have produced! Congratulations to you and your staff. You deserve the Nobel prize in Education. Thanks for helping me understand computers."

Bruno Tonon (Melbourne, Australia)

"A Picture Is Worth A Thousand Words! If your learning method is by observing or hands-on training, this is the book for you!"

Lorri Pegan-Durastante (Wickliffe, OH)

"Over time, I have bought a number of your 'Read Less - Learn More' books. For me, they are THE way to learn anything easily. I learn easiest using your method of teaching."

José A. Mazón (Cuba, NY)

"You've got a fan for life!! Thanks so much!!"

Kevin P. Quinn (Oakland, CA)

"I have several books from the Visual series and have always found them to be valuable resources."

Stephen P. Miller (Ballston Spa, NY)

"I have several of your Visual books and they are the best I have ever used."

Stanley Clark (Crawfordville, FL)

"Like a lot of other people, I understand things best when I see them visually. Your books really make learning easy and life more fun."

John T. Frey (Cadillac, MI)

"I have quite a few of your Visual books and have been very pleased with all of them. I love the way the lessons are presented!"

Mary Jane Newman (Yorba Linda, CA)

"Thank you, thank you, thank you...for making it so easy for me to break into this high-tech world."

Gay O'Donnell (Calgary, Alberta,Canada)

"I write to extend my thanks and appreciation for your books. They are clear, easy to follow, and straight to the point. Keep up the good work! I bought several of your books and they are just right! No regrets! I will always buy your books because they are the best."

Seward Kollie (Dakar, Senegal)

"I would like to take this time to thank you and your company for producing great and easy-to-learn products. I bought two of your books from a local bookstore, and it was the best investment I've ever made! Thank you for thinking of us ordinary people."

Jeff Eastman (West Des Moines, IA)

"Compliments to the chef!! Your books are extraordinary! Or, simply put, extra-ordinary, meaning way above the rest! THANKYOU THANKYOU THANKYOU! I buy them for friends, family, and colleagues."

Christine J. Manfrin (Castle Rock, CO)

CREDITS

Project Editor
Tim Borek

Acquisitions Editor
Jody Lefevere

Copy Editor
Scott Tullis

Technical Editor
Lee Musick

Editorial Manager
Robyn Siesky

Business Manager
Amy Knies

Editorial Assistant
Laura Sinise

Manufacturing
Allan Conley
Linda Cook
Paul Gilchrist
Jennifer Guynn

Indexer
Johnna VanHoose Dinse

Special Help:
Ronda David-Burroughs
Sarah Hellert

Book Design
Kathie S. Rickard

Production Coordinator
Adrienne Martinez

Layout
LeAndra Hosier
Amanda Spagnuolo

Screen Artists
Joyce Haughey
Jill A. Proll

Cover Design
Anthony Bunyan

Proofreader
Shannon Ramsey

Quality Control
Cynthia Fields

**Vice President and Executive
Group Publisher**
Richard Swadley

Vice President and Publisher
Barry Pruett

Composition Director
Debbie Stailey

Wiley Bicentennial Logo:
Richard J. Pacifico

ABOUT THE AUTHOR

Paul McFedries is the president of Logophilia Limited, a technical writing company. While now primarily a writer, Paul has worked as a programmer, consultant, and Web site developer. Paul has written nearly 50 books that have sold over three million copies worldwide. These books include the Wiley titles *The Unofficial Guide to Microsoft Office 2007, Teach Yourself VISUALLY Windows Vista, Windows Vista: Top 100 Simplified Tips and Tricks* and *Teach Yourself VISUALLY Computers*. Paul also runs Word Spy, a Web site dedicated to tracking new words and phrases (see www.wordspy.com).

HOW TO USE THIS BOOK

PowerPoint® 2007: Top 100 Simplified® Tips & Tricks includes 100 tasks that reveal cool secrets, teach timesaving tricks, and explain great tips guaranteed to make you more productive with PowerPoint. The easy-to-use layout lets you work through all the tasks from beginning to end or jump in at random.

Who is this book for?

You already know PowerPoint basics. Now you'd like to go beyond, with shortcuts, tricks and tips that let you work smarter and faster. And because you learn more easily when someone *shows* you how, this is the book for you.

Conventions Used In This Book

❶ Steps

This book uses step-by-step instructions to guide you easily through each task. Numbered callouts on every screen shot show you exactly how to perform each task, step by step.

❷ Tips

Practical tips provide insights to save you time and trouble, caution you about hazards to avoid, and reveal how to do things in PowerPoint that you never thought possible!

❸ Task Numbers

Task numbers from 1 to 100 indicate which lesson you are working on.

❹ Difficulty Levels

For quick reference, these symbols mark the difficulty level of each task.

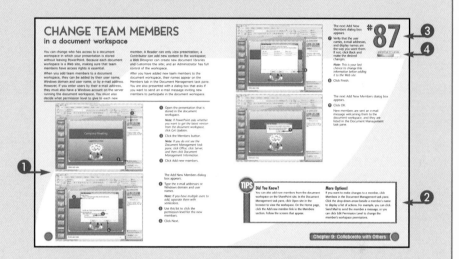

DIFFICULTY LEVEL	Demonstrates a new spin on a common task
DIFFICULTY LEVEL	Introduces a new skill or a new task
DIFFICULTY LEVEL	Combines multiple skills requiring in-depth knowledge
DIFFICULTY LEVEL	Requires extensive skill and may involve other technologies

Table of Contents

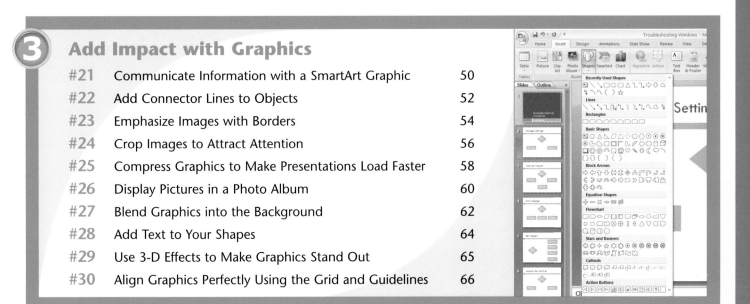

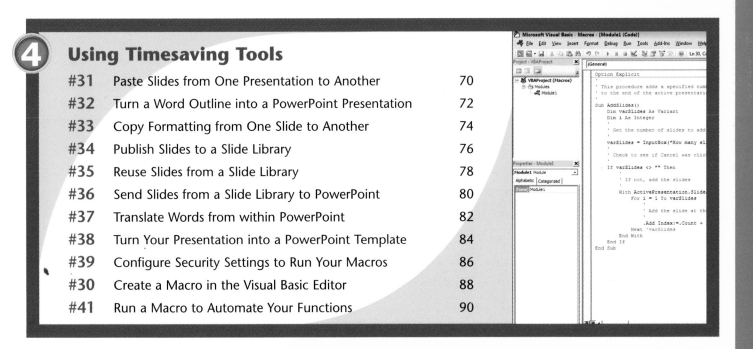

Table of Contents

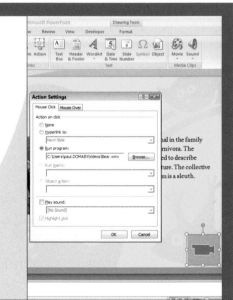

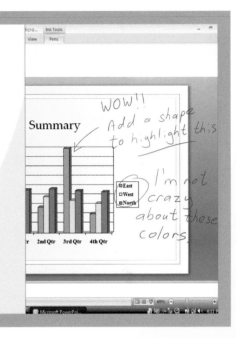

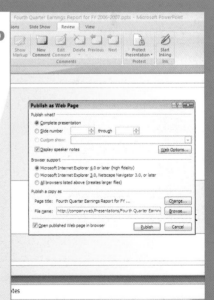

Table of Contents

Customize PowerPoint Options to Suit Your Needs

You can get more done and you can get it done faster with PowerPoint when you customize its options to suit your needs. The tasks in this chapter are geared toward making the PowerPoint user interface work for you by helping you to place the tools you need where you need them.

If you have ever wondered how to open presentations with the Outline tab showing or with the Notes Page hidden, find out how here. It only takes a few minutes to configure PowerPoint to open presentations in the view in which you are most comfortable.

If you are tired of browsing to file folders many levels deep to find or save files, you can save time by adding a shortcut to the Favorites links. You can customize the Quick Access

Toolbar to place the commands and features that you use most where they work best for you.

You can adjust various settings that streamline the way you use PowerPoint. For example, you can toggle the Mini toolbar and the Live Preview settings on and off, configure PowerPoint's ScreenTips, modify the PowerPoint color scheme, and change your user name. To ensure accurate spelling, you can also customize the spell checker as well as PowerPoint's AutoCorrect settings.

PowerPoint also offers a number of options that control slide shows, editing, printing, and AutoFormat, and you learn about those options in this chapter.

Top 100

CHANGE THE DEFAULT VIEW
of your presentation

You can view presentations in the format in which you are most comfortable when you change the default view in which presentations appear. For example, you may find that you routinely switch from the Slide tab to the Outline tab to see the organization of your presentation at a glance. On the other hand, you may find that you rarely use Notes, so you often turn off the Notes Page in order to concentrate on arranging your slides.

If you routinely change the way you view

presentations in PowerPoint, you can save time by specifying the default view you would like PowerPoint to use instead of making manual changes to the view each time you open a presentation. When you change the default view, PowerPoint displays only the parts of the screen that you want to see, such as the Outline or Slide tab, the Notes Page, or any combination of these options. After you specify the view you would like to use, you can see it take effect the next time you open a presentation.

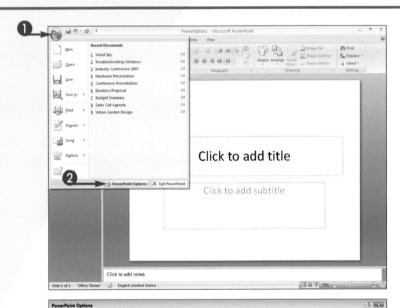

1 Click the Office button.

2 Click PowerPoint Options.

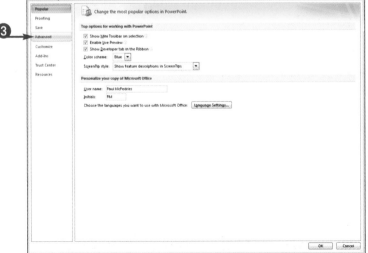

The PowerPoint Options dialog box opens.

3 Click Advanced.

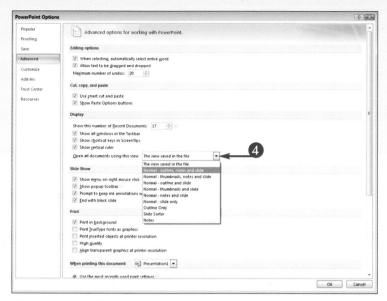

④ Click here and then select the view you want to use as the default.

DIFFICULTY LEVEL

⑤ Click OK.

The Options dialog box closes, and the next time a presentation is opened, the view is changed.

TIPS

Did You Know?

You can always change a presentation's view after you open it. For example, to view or remove the Notes Page, click View, and then click Notes Page.

Try This!

If you spend a lot of time reviewing presentations, you may want to set the default view to open presentations to the Slide Sorter. To do this, perform Steps **1** to **4** above and then click the Slide Sorter option from the drop-down menu.

Customize It!

You can open presentations in the view in which the file was saved. To do this, perform Steps **1** to **4** above, and then use the drop-down list to click the option named The view saved in the file.

ADD A SHORTCUT
to the Favorite Links

You can save time and access files quickly by adding a shortcut for commonly used folders to the Windows Vista Favorite Links list. The Favorite Links list appears on the Open and Save As dialog boxes and is most commonly used to access your Desktop, Documents, Computer, and Public folders.

Adding a shortcut to the Favorite Links list adds an icon to the list that represents a file folder, network location, or even a Web site. When you want to open a file from that location, you can simply click the shortcut to see the list of files that are available. Similarly, when you save a file, you can click the shortcut to save files directly to that location. You can also continue to browse folders even after you click the shortcut; shortcuts in the Favorite Links list are often used to quickly get to a hard drive or network drive and then locate the specific folder you want to use thereafter.

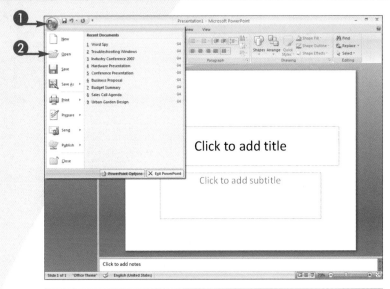

ADD THE SHORTCUT

1. Click the Office button.
2. Click Open.

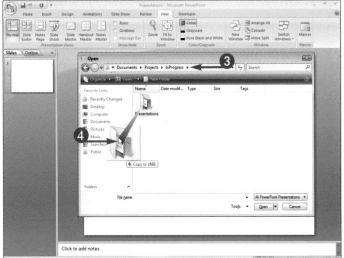

The Open dialog box appears.

3. Open the folder that contains the subfolder you want to add as a shortcut.

4. Click and drag the folder and drop it inside the Favorite Links list.

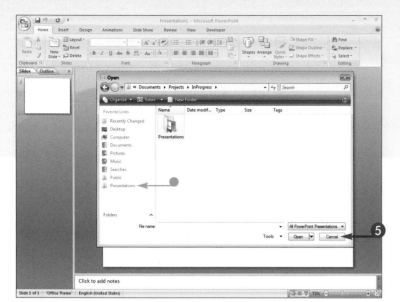

● The shortcut appears in the Favorite Links list.

⑤ Click Cancel.

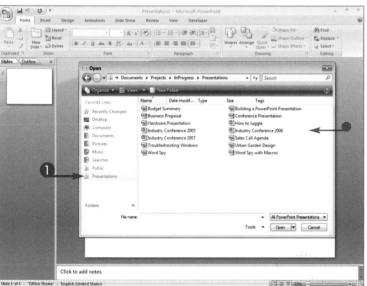

USE THE SHORTCUT

① In the Open or Save As dialog box, click the shortcut icon in the Favorite Links list.

● The folder opens.

TIPS

Did You Know?

Because all of the Microsoft Office 2007 programs use the Windows Vista Open and Save As dialog boxes, a shortcut you add to the Favorite Links list in PowerPoint is also accessible in other programs like Microsoft Word and Microsoft Excel.

Try This!

To create network shortcuts, display the Open or Save As dialog box, click Folders, click Network, and then double-click a computer to see its shared folders. You can then click and drag a shared folder to the Favorite Links list.

Cross-Platform

In Windows XP, add shortcuts to the My Places Bar, instead. In the Open or Save As dialog box, open the folder, click Tools, and then click Add to "My Places." The shortcut appears in the My Places Bar on the left side of the dialog box.

Customize the Quick Access toolbar for
EASIER COMMAND ACCESS

You can make your life easier and more efficient and you can get the most of the Quick Access toolbar by populating it with the commands that you use most often. The Quick Access toolbar appears to the right of the Office button in the upper left corner of PowerPoint. By default, this toolbar offers buttons for the three most frequently used commands: Save, Undo, and Repeat. If there are commands on the Ribbon that you use frequently, you can access them

even easier by placing them on the Quick Access toolbar. You can add any PowerPoint command to the Quick Access toolbar.

Note that you are not restricted to just a few commands. If you place the Quick Access toolbar below the Ribbon, you can use the full width of the window, plus you get a More Controls button at the end of the toolbar that enables you to display another whole row of commands.

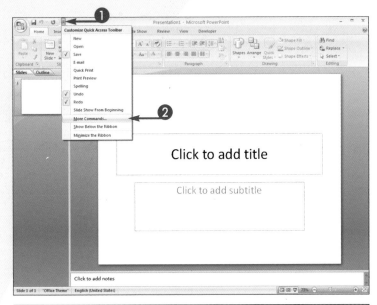

① Click the Customize Quick Access Toolbar button.

② Click More Commands.

The PowerPoint Options dialog box appears, with the Customization page displayed.

③ Click here and select a category that holds the command button to add to the toolbar.

④ Click the command to add.

⑤ Click Add.

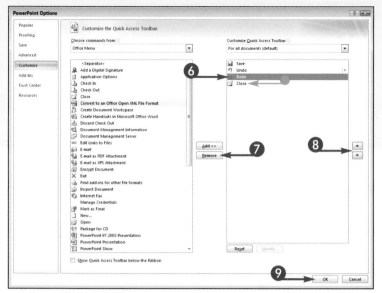

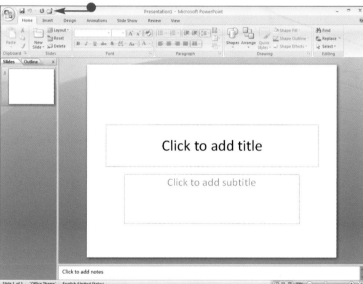

- The command appears on the list of commands currently available on the Quick Access toolbar.

6 Click a command to delete, move up, or move down in the list of commands currently on the toolbar.

7 Click Remove to remove it from the toolbar.

8 Click the Move Up or Move Down button to change a command's position.

9 Click OK.

- The PowerPoint Options dialog box closes, and the Quick Access toolbar shows its new command arrangement.

DIFFICULTY LEVEL

TIPS

Try This!
To move the Quick Access toolbar below the Ribbon, click the Customize Quick Access Toolbar button and then click Show Below the Ribbon. PowerPoint moves the toolbar under the Ribbon, which gives you more room to add commands.

More Options!
There is an easier way to add some commands to the Quick Access toolbar. Either pull down the Office menu or display the Ribbon tab that contains the command you want to add. Right-click the command and then click Add to Quick Access Toolbar.

Remove It!
To revert the Quick Access toolbar to its default state, click the Customize Quick Access Toolbar button, and then click More Commands. Click the Reset button and then click Yes in the Reset Customizations dialog box that appears. Click OK to return to PowerPoint.

Customize PowerPoint's
MOST POPULAR OPTIONS

PowerPoint maintains a collection of what it calls "popular options" for working with the program. You can improve a number of key aspects of PowerPoint by customizing these popular options to suit the way you prefer to work.

Some of these options are common to working with a variety of features. For example, the Mini toolbar appears when you select any text in PowerPoint, and it includes buttons for common text tasks, such as Bold and Font. Similarly, the ScreenTips appear when you hover the mouse pointer over any Ribbon object, and the Live Preview feature shows you a preview of how an option affects the slide. The popular options enable you to toggle each of these features on and off.

PowerPoint's popular options also include the program color scheme, your user name and initials, and the languages you want to use with PowerPoint. You can change these common options in the PowerPoint Options dialog box.

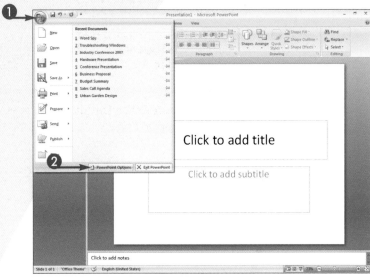

① Click the Office button.

② Click PowerPoint Options.

The PowerPoint Options dialog box appears.

③ Click Popular.

④ Make your choices in the Top options for working with PowerPoint section.

● Click the Show Mini Toolbar on selection check box to toggle the Mini toolbar.

● Click the Enable Live Preview check box to enable or disable Live Preview.

● You can click here and select the program color scheme.

● You can click here and select a style of ScreenTip to display.

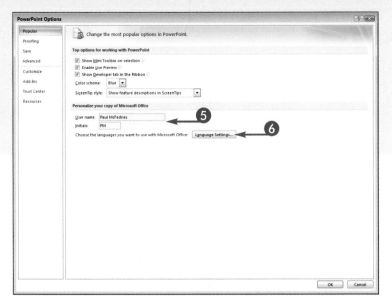

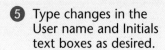

DIFFICULTY LEVEL

⑤ Type changes in the User name and Initials text boxes as desired.

When you create a file, PowerPoint uses the User name entry to identify you as the file's author.

⑥ Click Language Settings.

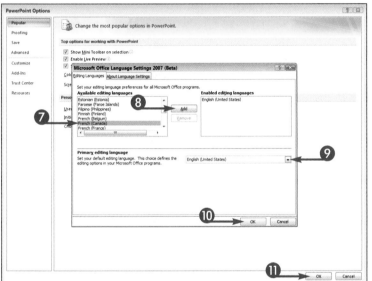

⑦ Click an editing language.

⑧ Click Add.

PowerPoint adds the language to the list of enabled editing languages.

⑨ Click here and select a primary editing language if the language shown is different from the language you use most.

⑩ Click OK.

The Microsoft Office Language Settings dialog box closes.

⑪ Click OK.

PowerPoint applies your new settings.

More Options!
If you activate the Show Developer Tab check box, PowerPoint adds a Developer tab to the Ribbon. That tab offers choices for writing PowerPoint macros. If you later learn macro programming skills, you can use the tools on the Developer tab to not only create macros, but also to apply those macros to controls such as buttons and list boxes that you add to slides.

Did You Know?
PowerPoint takes the User name setting and applies it to the Author property for each new presentation you create. However, you can change the Author property at any time: Click Office, click Prepare, and then click Properties. In the Document Information Panel that appears, edit the Author text box as required. When you are done, click the Document Information Panel's Close button.

Customize how PowerPoint
SAVES YOUR PRESENTATIONS

You can safeguard your work and make presentation files easier to share with other people by customizing PowerPoint's save options. For example, PowerPoint saves presentations in the PowerPoint 2007 file format. If you often share your presentations with a colleague who uses an older PowerPoint version, you can set the PowerPoint Presentation 97–2003 file format as the default. Similarly, you can also change the default location where PowerPoint saves your files. For example, you might want to save your presentations to a folder shared on your network,

which enables other people to access, view, and collaborate on the presentations.

To help ensure that you do not lose work, PowerPoint automatically saves AutoRecover information every 10 minutes. If PowerPoint or Windows crashes, PowerPoint uses the AutoRecover data to restore changes you made since you last saved the file. Unfortunately, this interval may still mean that you lose work if you are a fast worker. To reduce the chance that you lose work, you can reduce the AutoRecover interval to make your work even safer.

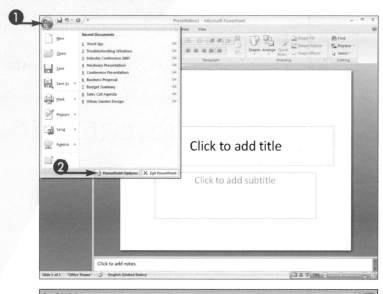

1 Click the Office button.

2 Click PowerPoint Options.

The PowerPoint Options dialog box appears.

3 Click Save.

4 Click here and select a file format.

When you later save a new file, PowerPoint will by default use the specified format unless you choose another format in the Save As dialog box.

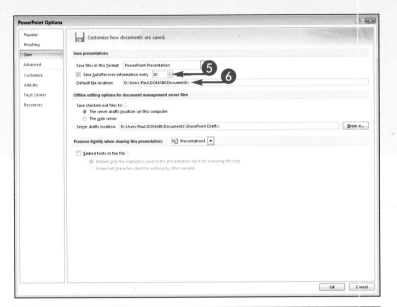

5 If desired, use the text box or the spin box buttons to change the number of minutes between saving AutoRecover information.

Note: *Clicking the Save AutoRecover information check box to clear it turns off auto saving.*

6 If you want to save presentation files to a particular folder that's different than PowerPoint's default, edit the Default file location text box entry.

7 Click Embed fonts in the file.

PowerPoint now saves fonts in the presentation file so that the presentation appears the same when viewed on a system lacking the fonts used in the presentation.

● You can further specify whether to embed all characters or only those in use.

8 Click OK.

The dialog box closes and PowerPoint applies the new save settings.

#5

DIFFICULTY LEVEL

Did You Know?

Fonts install with the Windows operating system and programs like Microsoft Office. Fonts such as Book Antiqua or Garamond are not available to every computer. If you use a particular font in a presentation and do not embed it, PowerPoint will replace it with a base font, which may throw off the presentation design.

Caution!

If you only work with small presentations, you can set a short AutoRecover interval, such as 1 or 2 minutes. However, if you often work with large presentations, PowerPoint can take a while to save such files. This means that a short AutoRecover interval will only slow you down. In this case, an interval around 5 minutes is often a good compromise between speed and safety.

Modify the
DISPLAY AND SLIDE
SHOW OPTIONS

You can use PowerPoint's display options to customize the display of elements in the PowerPoint window. For example, PowerPoint enables you to specify the number of documents that appear on the Office menu's Recent Documents list. The default number of documents is 17, but you can display up to 50 documents. (If your screen is not big enough to display the number of documents that you specify, PowerPoint just displays as many as it can.) You can also specify whether PowerPoint displays taskbar buttons for each open presentation, includes shortcut

keys in the ScreenTips, and displays the vertical ruler.

You can also use PowerPoint's slide show options to customize the defaults for running slide shows. For example, you can control whether a menu appears when you right-click the screen during the slide show, whether the toolbar appears during slide show playback, whether PowerPoint prompts you to keep ink annotations at the end of the show, and whether PowerPoint ends slide shows with a black slide.

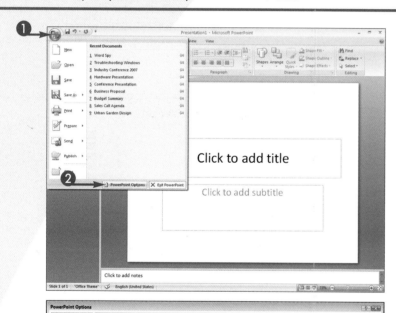

1 Click the Office button.

2 Click PowerPoint Options.

The PowerPoint Options dialog box appears.

3 Click Advanced.

4 Use the Display section to specify your desired choices affecting how PowerPoint displays presentations.

● You can use the text box or click the spin box buttons to change the number of files displayed in the Recent Documents list.

● You can click the Show all windows in the Taskbar check box to toggle presentation taskbar buttons on and off.

● You can click the Show shortcut keys in ScreenTips check box to toggle ScreenTip shortcut keys on and off.

14

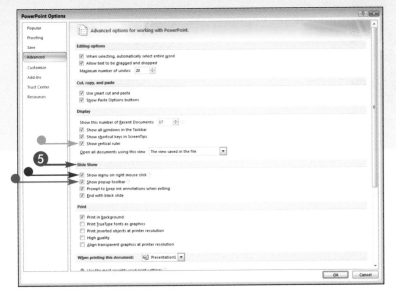

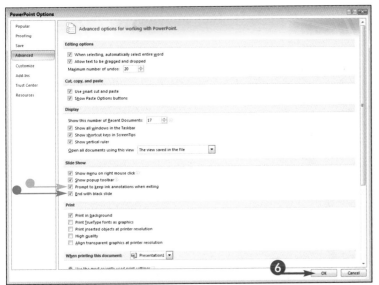

- You can click the Show vertical ruler check box to toggle the vertical ruler on and off.

⑤ Use the Slide Show section to make your desired choices affecting slide shows.

- You can click the Show menu on right mouse click check box to toggle the right-click menu on and off.

- You can click the Show popup toolbar check box to toggle the navigation toolbar on and off.

- You can click the Prompt to keep ink annotations when exiting check box to toggle the ink prompt on and off.

- You can click the End with black slide check box to toggle the ending black slide on and off.

⑥ Click OK.

The dialog box closes and PowerPoint applies the new settings.

TIPS

Caution!

If you deactivate the Prompt to keep ink annotations when exiting check box, PowerPoint does not give you any way to save your annotations. The only way to save annotations is via the dialog box that appears at the end of the slide show to prompt you to save them. With that check box deselected in the PowerPoint Options dialog box, you can no longer save annotations.

Did You Know?

You see only the vertical ruler when you enable PowerPoint's Ruler option. To activate this feature, click View and then click the Ruler check box. (You can also right-click the current slide or slide background and then click Ruler.) PowerPoint displays the Ruler. If you deactivated the Show vertical ruler check box, PowerPoint displays only the horizontal ruler.

Change the
EDITING SETTINGS

You can customize PowerPoint's editing options to suit the way you work. For example, when you quickly drag your mouse across text to select it, PowerPoint automatically selects each word as you reach it. You can turn off this feature if you more often select only partial words. You can also turn off PowerPoint's feature that enables you to drag and drop text.

If you often use the Undo feature, you can customize the number of operations that you can undo. The default is 20, but you can go as high as 150. PowerPoint also enables you to turn off the smart cut and paste feature, which automatically adds spaces when you paste text. Finally, you also can control the use of more recent features such as the Paste Options button, which appears when you paste a cut or copied object. Click it to see commands for working with the pasted selection.

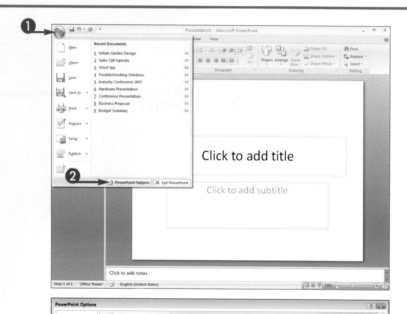

① Click the Office button.

② Click PowerPoint Options.

The PowerPoint Options dialog box appears.

③ Click Advanced.

④ Make the choices you prefer in the Editing options section.

● You can click this check box to enable or disable the automatic selection of an entire word.

● You can click this check box to enable or disable text drag-and-drop.

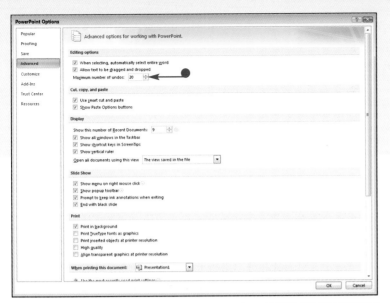

● You can use the Maximum number of undos text box or spin box buttons to change the number of operations that you can undo.

DIFFICULTY LEVEL

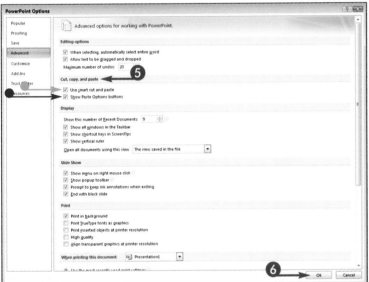

⑤ Select Cut, copy, and paste options.

● You can click to enable or disable smart cut and paste.

● You can click this check box to enable or disable the Paste Options buttons.

⑥ Click OK.

The dialog box closes, and PowerPoint applies the changes.

TIPS

Did You Know?

The Paste Options button appears below a pasted object. It offers formatting options such as retaining the original source formatting. Smart cut and paste helps to eliminate errors that can happen when you paste text or an object. Sometimes, if no spacing was selected around the cut or copied selection, it bumps up against other text when pasted. Smart cut and paste inserts missing space when pasted to eliminate that problem.

Caution!

Be careful with the Maximum number of undos setting. When you set this number quite high — say, over 100 — PowerPoint usually requires lots of system memory to store so many undo operations. If you feel that PowerPoint's performance is slow, consider lowering the number of undos.

Work with the
PRINT OPTIONS

Most presentations exist only as electronic files. You create, work on, and save the presentation on your computer, and you may transfer the presentation file to a notebook computer for the presentation itself. The days of projecting overhead transparencies using acetate sheets may not be completely over, but thanks to PowerPoint their days are numbered.

When you do need hardcopy, however, you can customize presentation printing by modifying the print options. For example, you can configure PowerPoint to print in the background so that you can keep on working while the print job runs. You

can also print TrueType fonts as graphics, which speeds up printing if your printer supports this feature. Also, you can print inserted graphics at the printer's resolution, which improves the look of slide images.

You also can specify that a particular presentation always be printed with a particular printer and settings. These settings include what you want printed, whether you use color, grayscale, or black and white, and whether you print hidden slides, scale slides to fit the paper, and frame the slides.

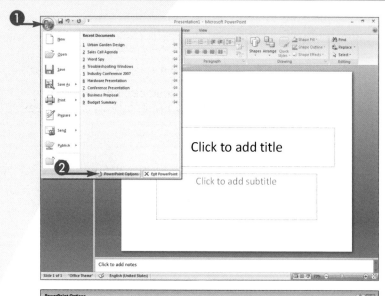

① Click the Office button.

② Click PowerPoint Options.

The PowerPoint Options dialog box appears.

③ Click Advanced.

④ Make the choices you prefer in the Print section.

● You can click this check box to enable or disable background printing.

● You can click this check box to enable or disable printing TrueType fonts as graphics.

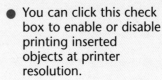

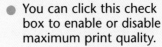

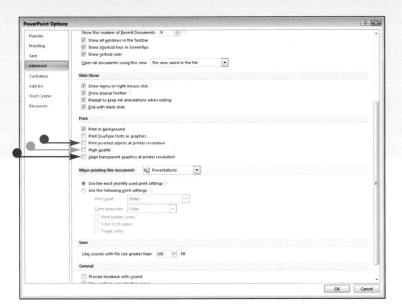

- You can click this check box to enable or disable printing inserted objects at printer resolution.

- You can click this check box to enable or disable maximum print quality.

- You can click this check box to enable or disable the alignment of transparent content with other slide content.

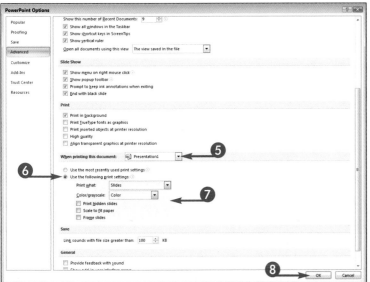

⑤ Use the When printing this document list to click an open presentation file for which you want to set particular print settings.

⑥ Click Use the following print settings option (◎ changes to ◉).

The rest of the choices become available.

⑦ Click the desired settings for printing the selected presentation (☐ changes to ☑).

⑧ Click OK.

The dialog box closes and PowerPoint applies the new settings.

Try This!

If you find that your presentations print slowly, you can try a couple of things. Enabling the Print in background option can slow down your computer, so you can try turning that feature off by clicking it to clear its check box. Also, inserting graphic files with a low resolution but having Print inserted objects at printer resolution checked would actually slow down the printer because it would require increasing the graphics' resolutions.

Did You Know?

If you use a background color, pattern, texture, or image, the background appears to come to an abrupt halt at the edges of each slide, which can make slides look artificial. You can overcome this problem by activating the Frame slides check box. PowerPoint then *frames* the slides, which puts a thin border around the edges of each slide. This helps to "contain" the background, which makes your printouts more attractive.

Change the
AUTOFORMAT SETTINGS

You can customize PowerPoint's AutoFormat As You Type settings for increased efficiency as well as to suit the way you work. The AutoFormat feature works much like AutoCorrect, except that it corrects text formatting rather than text spelling. For example, AutoFormat automatically replaces regular quotes with smart quotes; fractions written as separate characters (such as 1/2) with fraction symbols (such as $\frac{1}{2}$); ordinals (such as 1st) with superscripts (such as 1st); two hyphens (--) with an em dash (—); smiley faces and arrows (such as :-)

and ==>) with equivalent symbols (such as ☺ and →); and Internet and network addresses with hyperlinks to those locations.

AutoFormat also applies formatting automatically. For example, AutoFormat automatically converts lists of items to bulleted or numbered lists. AutoFormat also automatically fits title text and body text to their placeholders. You can turn these formatting changes off and back on as needed.

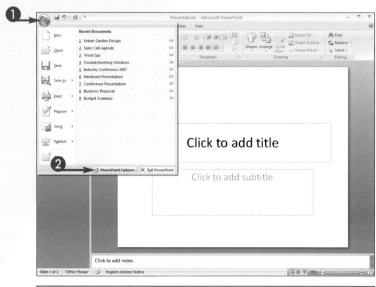

① Click the Office button.

② Click PowerPoint Options.

The PowerPoint Options dialog box appears.

③ Click Proofing.

④ Click the AutoCorrect Options button.

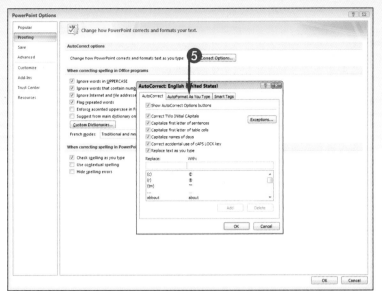

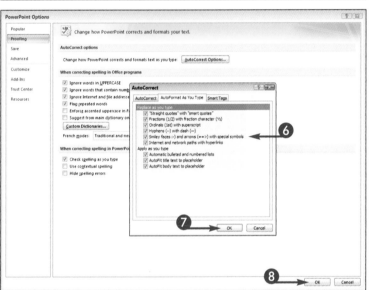

The AutoCorrect dialog box appears.

5 Click the AutoFormat As You Type tab.

DIFFICULTY LEVEL

6 Click any formatting choice — uncheck it to disable it or recheck it to enable it.

7 Click OK.

The AutoCorrect dialog box closes.

8 Click OK.

The PowerPoint Options dialog box closes, applying the new settings.

Try This!

It does not make sense to turn off the AutoFormat As You Type options and then turn them back on when you need them. A better strategy is to leave these options activated. If PowerPoint then applies an AutoFormat that you do not want to use, press Ctrl+Z to restore the text.

More Options!

Smart tags identify certain types of text with an underline. When you position the mouse pointer over the text, such as a date, the smart tag appears, and you can click it to see a list of actions associated with the text, such as scheduling a meeting. In the Smart Tags tab, click the Label text with smart tags check box to activate this feature.

Chapter 2

Give Your Presentation the Look You Want

You can use tools in PowerPoint 2007 to give your presentations a professional look that gets your work noticed. For example, you can customize any of PowerPoint's built-in layouts by removing any of the predefined content placeholders.

You can also give your presentations a consistent format across presentations by using Slide Masters. You can create your own Slide Masters to suit your unique formatting needs.

You can emphasize a key message or logo when you place watermark text or a watermark image in the background of a printed slide. You can also place slide numbers on each slide in a presentation to make it easier for audience members to find particular slides.

If you are looking for ways to provide consistency across presentations, printed materials, and Web sites, you can find out how to change the fonts used throughout an entire presentation. You can use custom graphics or other materials from a Web site as bullets in your presentations or background images for slides. You can also quickly change the layout of slides whenever needed. PowerPoint 2007 also enables you to apply colors to various elements and then save those colors as a custom color scheme.

If you work with international customers, partners, or co-workers, you can enable the display and editing of content in a wide variety of languages to expand the impact of your presentation.

Top 100

CUSTOMIZE A LAYOUT

by removing placeholders

You can customize a particular slide layout by removing a placeholder from that layout using the Slide Master view.

The layouts in the Slide Master contain placeholders for the slide title, text or graphic content, date, footer, and slide numbers. If you are not using a particular placeholder, you may prefer to remove it from the slide layout in the master.

Note that deleting the title or text placeholder from the slide master layout at the top does not delete the title from other slide layouts. When you work with a particular layout in the Slide Master view, any changes you make apply only to that layout.

After you change the Slide Master and close the view, PowerPoint redisplays whatever view you had open previously — either Normal view or Slide Sorter view. Your global changes appear there.

Bear in mind, as well, that when you apply a document theme to your presentation, PowerPoint automatically creates a set of slide masters containing all the settings for that theme.

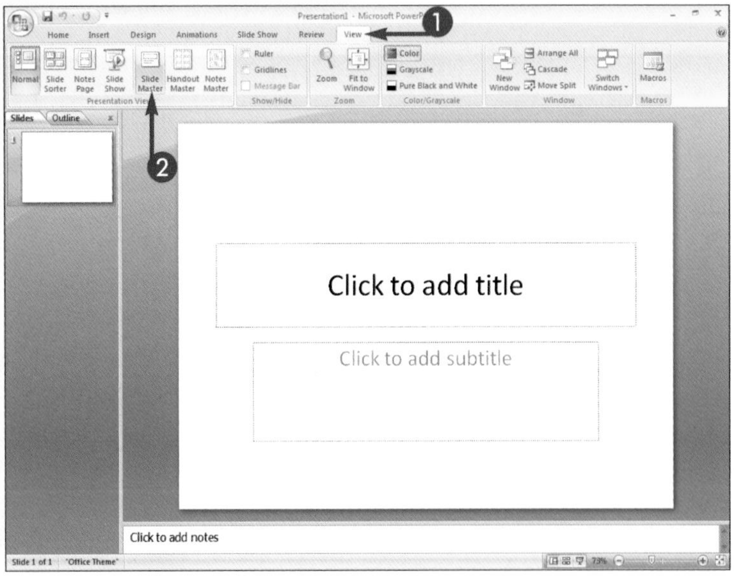

Display the Slide Master View

1. Click the View tab.
2. Click Slide Master.

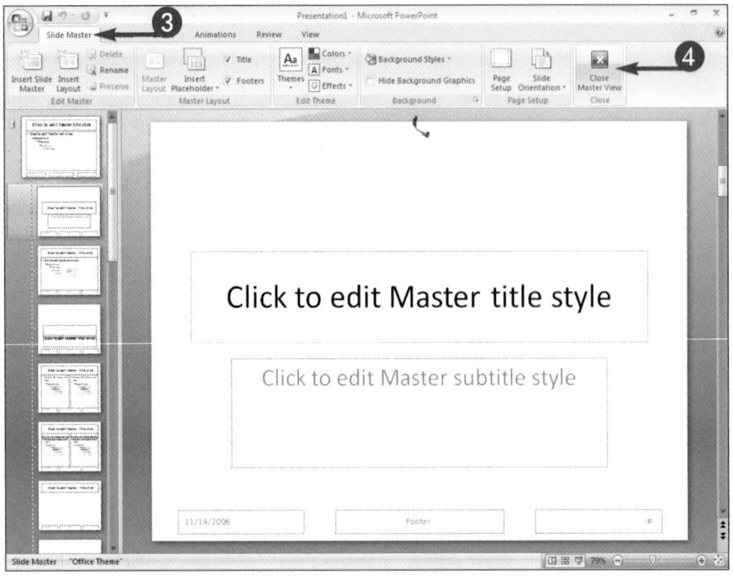

PowerPoint switches to Slide Master view.

3. Click the Slide Master tab, if needed.
4. When you have completed your work in Slide Master view, click Close Master View.

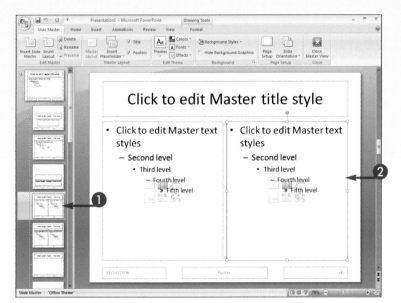

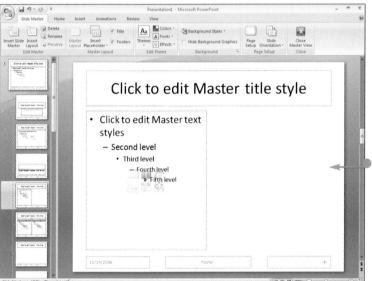

① With Slide Master view displayed, click the layout containing the placeholder you want to remove.

② Click the placeholder you want to delete.

PowerPoint selects the placeholder.

③ Press Delete.

DIFFICULTY LEVEL

● The placeholder disappears.

Did You Know?
If you delete a placeholder from a layout, only the placeholder is removed from slides already using that layout. Any content you inserted into that placeholder on a slide remains in place. Slides added to the presentation after you remove the placeholder from the master will no longer have the placeholder.

Caution!
Be careful when you delete a footer placeholder or a date/time placeholder from the Slide Master or a layout master. If you delete the placeholder for footer, date, or time but then later display that information, it will appear on the slide or may appear in an unexpected location.

Change layouts when you
CREATE YOUR OWN MASTERS

You can change the look of all of the slides in your presentation when you create a new Slide Master. Slide Masters are templates that define how slides are formatted. Slide Masters also allow you to insert common elements on every slide, such as slide number, the date, footer text, or even logos or pictures. If you want all of the slides in your presentation to use similar fonts, formatting, and graphics, Slide Masters are the best way to do this.

You may want to create a new Slide Master instead

of editing the existing one if you want to apply it only to selected slides or if you plan to use it only for a short time. You may also want to create a new Slide Master, and then apply it to the main Slide Master after you are sure how you want it. This task explains how to create a new Slide Master from an existing one, and then apply it to a slide or a presentation.

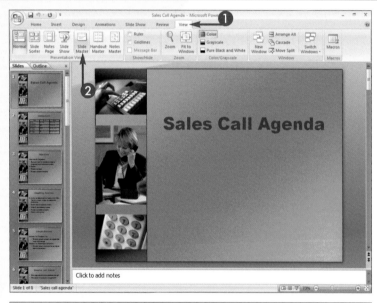

① Click the View tab.

② Click Slide Master.

PowerPoint switches to Slide Master view.

③ Right-click the Slide Master.

④ Click Duplicate Slide Master.

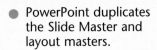
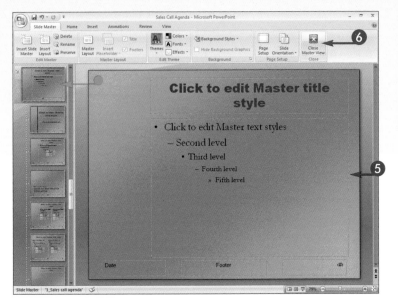

● PowerPoint duplicates the Slide Master and layout masters.

5 Edit and format the new Slide Master as desired.

6 When you finish editing the Slide Master, click Close Master View.

The Normal View of your presentation appears.

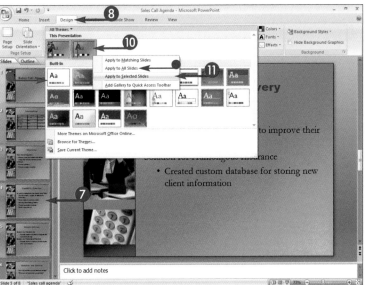

7 Select the slides to which you want to apply the new Slide Master.

8 Click the Design tab.

9 In the Themes group, click the Themes gallery's down arrow.

● PowerPoint displays the Themes gallery.

10 Right-click the new Slide Master.

11 Click Apply to Selected Slides.

● To apply the new Slide Master to every slide, click Apply to All Slides.

PowerPoint applies the new Slide Master.

Did You Know?

If you try to make changes to the new Slide Master, but PowerPoint does not apply those changes, it is likely that the new Slide Master has its "preserve" setting activated. To turn off this setting, click the new Slide Master, click the Slide Master tab, and then click Preserve. If PowerPoint asks whether you want to delete unused masters, click No.

More Options!

When you create the new Slide Master, PowerPoint gives it the same name as the original Slide Master, but with "1_" appended to the front of the name. To change the name of the new Slide Master, click View, click Slide Master, click the new Slide Master, and then click Rename. In the Rename Master dialog box, type the new name and then click OK.

ADD A WATERMARK
to your slides

You can communicate an important message or display a key image behind the text when you add watermarks to your presentations. Watermarks are commonly used to identify documents as a *draft*, as *confidential*, or with other messages. You can use watermarks to reinforce branding and corporate images by placing logos or marketing taglines behind text. Watermarks are most effective when they communicate the intended message without interfering with the slide. This is usually accomplished by using subtle colors that maintain the legibility of slide content.

You can apply a watermark to every slide by using the Slide Master, or you can apply different watermarks to selected slides. In each case, note that watermarks are different from the graphics and text you insert into your presentation because the watermarks appear and print behind your regular slide content.

You can easily create attention-getting watermarks by using the tools available in the Insert tab. You can create Shapes like callouts, stars, and banners, and insert text in them to deliver your messages. You can also insert text boxes, pictures, clip art, WordArt, and diagram objects that you can rotate or reformat however you choose.

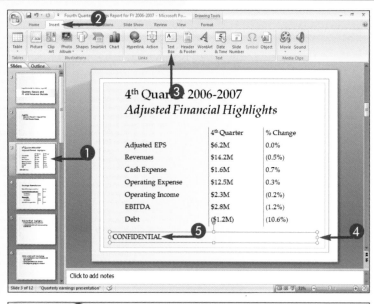

❶ Click the slide you want to work with.

If you want to apply the watermark to all the slides, click the View tab, click Slide Master, and then apply the watermark to the Slide Master, instead.

❷ Click the Insert tab.

❸ Click Text Box.

You can also click any of the object types in the Illustrations group.

❹ Click and drag to create the text box on the slide.

❺ Type your text.

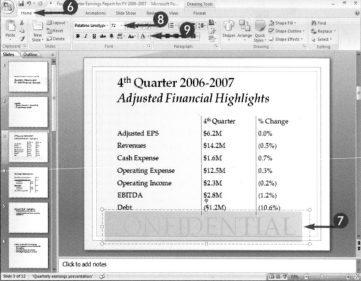

❻ Click the Home tab.

❼ Select the text.

❽ Click here and select the font size.

❾ Click here and select a light color.

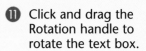

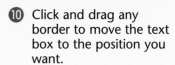

#12

DIFFICULTY LEVEL

⑩ Click and drag any border to move the text box to the position you want.

⑪ Click and drag the Rotation handle to rotate the text box.

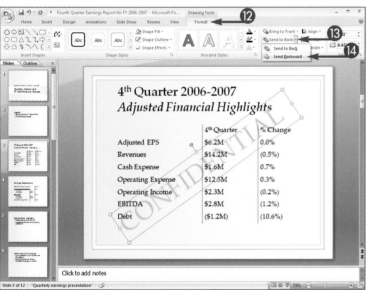

⑫ Click the Format tab.

⑬ Click Send to Back.

⑭ Click Send Backward.

PowerPoint sends the text box behind the slide content.

TIPS

More Options!

If you want to use a picture as a watermark, you need to wash out the image so that it does not interfere with the slide content. After you insert the image, click it, click the Format tab, click Recolor, and then click Washout. Remember, as well, to send the image behind the slide content: click Format, click the Send to Back arrow, and then click Send Backward.

Did You Know?

You can use Print Preview to see how your watermarks will look when printed. You can access Print Preview by clicking Office, then the Print arrow, and then Print Preview. It is a good idea to confirm how pages will print because pages with slides that cover the majority of the page will leave much of the watermark covered.

PLACE SLIDE NUMBERS
on all slides

You can insert numbers on slides to make them easier for audience members to reference. You may already be accustomed to placing page numbers on Slide, Handout, and Notes pages so that anyone following a printed copy of your presentation can easily find referenced pages. However, inserting numbers on slides enables audience members to ask questions about specific slides regardless of whether the audience member is looking at a Handout page printed with six slides per page or a Notes page that includes only one slide per page. Similarly, if an

audience member wants to ask a question about a slide and there are multiple slides with similar titles, adding slide numbers makes it easier for a viewer to ask about a specific slide.

Slide numbers are included on Notes and Handout pages by default, but they are not turned on for slides by default. This task explains how to add numbers to all slides in a presentation, and then how to edit slide number formatting.

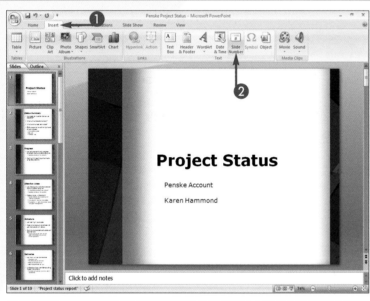

① Click the Insert tab.

② Click Slide Number.

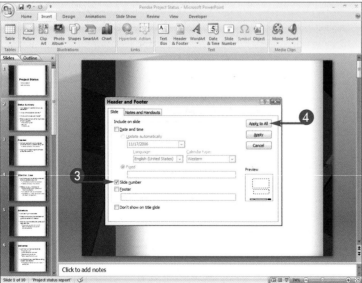

The Header and Footer dialog box appears.

③ Click the Slide number check box (changes to ✓).

④ Click Apply to All.

The Header and Footer dialog box closes.

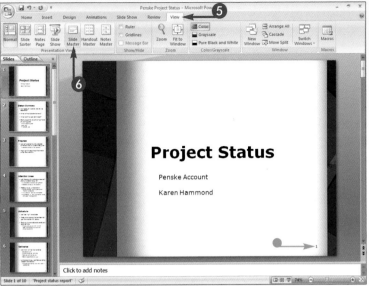

● PowerPoint applies the page number to all pages in the format specified in the Slide Master.

⑤ Click the View tab.

⑥ Click Slide Master.

The Slide Master view appears.

⑦ Select the slide number symbol (#).

⑧ Click the Home tab.

⑨ Use the controls in the Font group to format the slide number.

⑩ Click the Normal button.

PowerPoint closes Slide Master view and applies the slide number formatting to all slides.

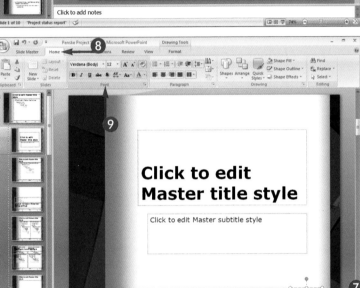

Did You Know?

Slide numbers that you add to the slides in your presentation also appear when you print your slides.

Apply It!

After you insert numbers into your slides, view them in Slide Show Mode to make sure that they are clearly visible. You can access Slide Show Mode by clicking Slide Show and then From Beginning. You can use Print Preview to see how the page numbers will look when they are printed by clicking Office, then the Print arrow, then Print Preview.

Did You Know?

You can easily insert slide numbers into individual slides instead of all slides. Follow Steps **1** to **3** above, but instead of clicking Apply to All in Step **4**, click Apply.

REPLACE ALL INSTANCES OF A FONT in your presentation

You can give your presentation a completely different look by replacing the fonts used in your presentation. Font replacements can transform a presentation from casual to professional to classic to formal.

Replacing every instance of a particular font can be especially useful when you have chosen to use a Design Template that has the look and feel you like, but which uses an unappealing font or a font that is different from what your company normally uses. Replacing a font can help ensure consistency with other materials you produce, such as written reports.

You can change fonts used throughout your presentation by changing the fonts in the Masters that control the formatting of your presentation. However, changing fonts in Slide Masters does not affect text in items not controlled by the Masters, such as text boxes. If you want to change fonts throughout your presentation, including in Masters, text boxes, and more, you can use Replace Fonts to replace one font with another. This task explains how selected fonts can be changed by using Replace Fonts to globally replace one font used in your presentation with another.

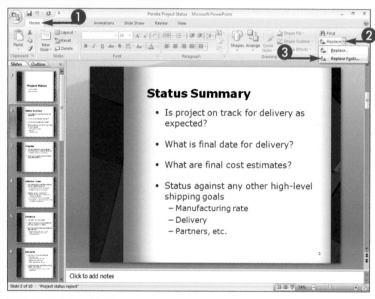

① Click the Home tab.

② Click Replace.

③ Click Replace Fonts.

The Replace Font dialog box appears.

④ Click the Replace drop-down menu.

⑤ Click the font you want to replace.

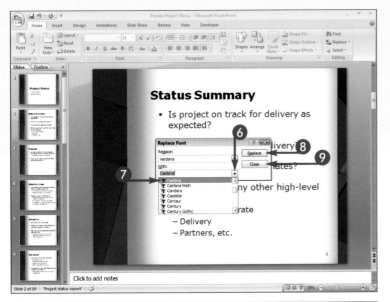

6 Click the With drop-down menu.

7 Click the font with which you want to replace the existing font.

8 Click Replace.

9 Click Close.

DIFFICULTY LEVEL

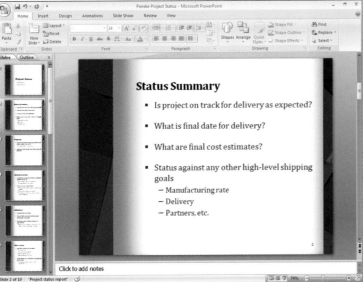

The font is replaced throughout the entire presentation.

TIPS

Caution!

Replace Fonts changes the font used everywhere in your presentation, including in Masters. Therefore, even if you select text that is 12-point Arial and use Replace Fonts to change it to Georgia, every instance of the Arial font will change to Georgia. Because the changes made with Replace Fonts are global, use this tool with caution.

Did You Know?

If you want to change fonts on elements that are controlled by a Slide Master, but only want those changes to apply to specific slides, you can create a new Slide Master to apply to selected slides. See Task #11 for information about how to create a new Slide Master.

MAKE A DOCUMENT THEME
THE DEFAULT for new presentations

You can most easily apply a theme that you use regularly by making that theme the default PowerPoint theme for new presentations.

If you applied a color theme, font theme, and background that really work together, you can save that combination as a new document theme that you can apply to other presentations. This is useful because it saves you the trouble of having to reapply the same custom colors, fonts, effects, and backgrounds the next time you want the same look.

After you have saved your custom theme, you can then set it as the default theme, which is the one that PowerPoint automatically applies to every new presentation. The standard default theme applies to each new presentation a blank background as well as the Calibri font in varying sizes depending on the placeholder. You may find that you constantly change this standard theme to some other theme. Although it is easy to change themes at any time, you can save time by configuring PowerPoint to use that theme as the default for all new presentations.

SAVE THE CUSTOM DOCUMENT THEME

① Click the Design tab.

② Use the Themes group to apply custom colors, fonts, and effects.

Note: To learn how to create a custom color scheme, see Task #20.

③ In the Themes group, click the Themes gallery's down arrow.

The Themes gallery appears.

④ Click Save Current Theme.

The Save Current Theme dialog box appears.

⑤ Type a filename.

There's no need to change the save folder. Using the default location ensures that the custom theme will show up in the gallery of themes.

⑥ Click Save.

PowerPoint adds the theme to the gallery in a special section labeled Custom.

SET THE CUSTOM THEME AS THE DEFAULT

1 Click the Design tab.

2 In the Themes group, click the Themes gallery's down arrow.

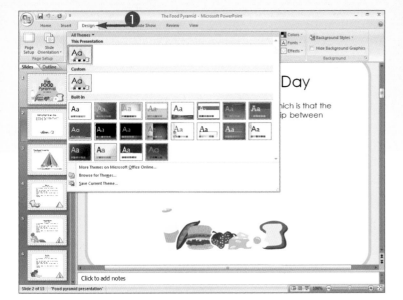

The gallery of themes appears.

3 Right-click the theme you want to set as the default.

4 Click Set as Default Theme.

The theme immediately becomes the default theme. Any blank presentation you create will use that theme.

TIPS

Reverse It!

The original default theme is called Office Theme. To return this theme as the default, click the Design tab and then, in the Themes group, click More to display the Themes gallery. In the Built-In section, find the Office Theme, right-click it, and then click Set as Default. If you have trouble finding the theme, point to a theme in the gallery, and a ScreenTip with the theme name pops up.

Remove It!

If you no longer require a custom theme, you can delete it to reduce clutter in the Document Themes folder. Click the Design tab and then, in the Themes group, click More to display the Themes gallery. In the Custom section, right-click the theme you want to remove, and then click Delete. When PowerPoint asks you to confirm the deletion, click Yes.

CREATE UNIQUE BULLETS
from your own custom graphics

You can give your presentations the look you want when you use your own custom graphics for bullets. Bullets are the graphical elements placed before text in most slides. Each level in most presentations uses different bullets, or different sized bullets. Therefore, you may want to import and then use various graphics files for each level of content in your presentation.

You can use custom bullets that you create with a graphics program or the bullets that you use on your Web site in your presentations. Using consistent

graphics across all of the documents you create, as well as the presentations you produce, helps reinforce your company's brand and image with a unified look.

The graphics files from which you create bullets can be in any file format PowerPoint supports, which includes virtually all of the most popular graphics files. After you use a custom graphics file as a picture bullet, it continues to be accessible from the Picture Bullets library for other projects.

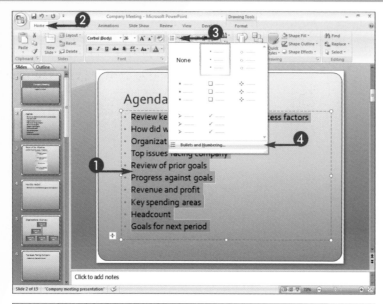

① Click and drag to select the text next to the bullets you want to change.

② Click the Home tab.

③ Click the Bullets menu.

④ Click Bullets and Numbering.

The Bullets and Numbering dialog box appears.

⑤ Click Picture.

The Picture Bullet dialog box appears.

⑥ Click Import.

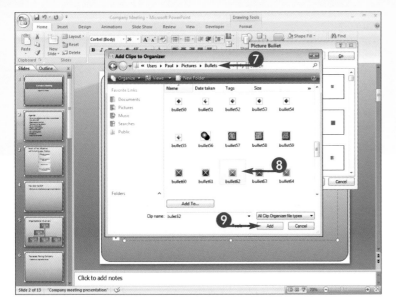

The Add Clips to Organizer dialog box appears.

⑦ Click here to locate the folder where your graphic files are stored.

⑧ Click the name of the graphic file you want to use in place of the current bullet.

⑨ Click Add.

DIFFICULTY LEVEL

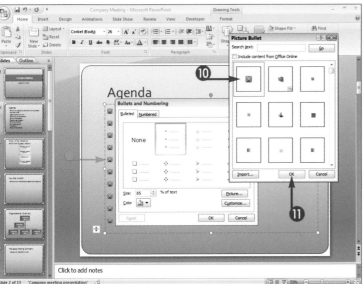

The Picture Bullet dialog box appears.

⑩ Click your custom bullet.

⑪ Click OK.

The Picture Bullet and Bullets and Numbering dialog boxes close.

● The presentation is updated with the new custom bullet.

TIPS

Apply It!
You can easily change the bullets throughout your presentation by altering the bullets used in the Slide Master. To access the Slide Master, click View and then Slide Master. Edit the bullets by following Steps 1 to 11 above and then click Close Master View. All of the slides using that Master are updated with your custom bullets.

Did You Know?
You can run presentations faster when you make sure the graphics files that you use are not large. Instead of using bullets that are uncompressed, such as BMP or TIF files, try using smaller, compressed graphics formats, such as JPEG or GIF files.

CHANGE THE LAYOUT
of an existing slide

You can freely change the layout of elements such as text, bulleted lists, graphics, buttons, animations, audio or video clips, and more on your slides whenever you want. You can easily click and drag elements to move them, or insert items like diagrams, graphs, and charts where needed. Better yet, you can save time when you use Slide Layouts to add elements and rearrange existing items without clicking and dragging and resizing elements on the slide.

The Slide Layout gallery gives you a clear visual representation of the many available layouts so you can quickly identify the right layout for your content. You can use the Slide Layout gallery to apply a layout to a selected slide or to a new slide. After the layout has been applied to the slide, you can easily insert pictures, text, audio, video, and more, and that content is placed according to your Slide Layout choices. If your content dictates a change in layout, you can easily choose from one of the other layouts whenever you want.

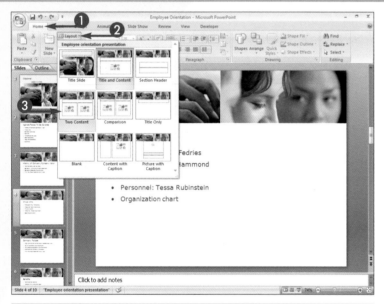

1 Click the Home tab.

2 Click Layout.

The Slide Layout gallery appears.

3 Click the slide layout that you want to apply.

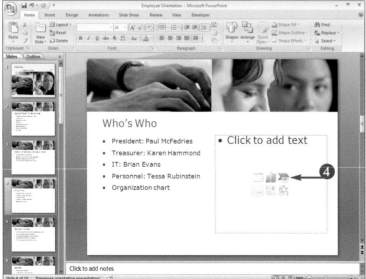

PowerPoint applies the new slide layout.

4 Click one of the icons to insert a table, a chart, a picture, a diagram, or a video clip.

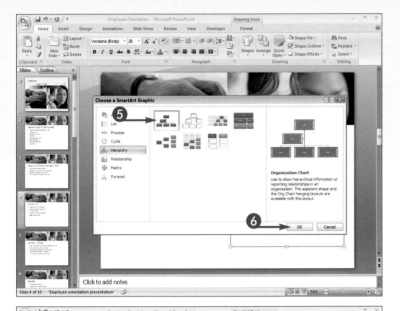

The appropriate dialog box opens.

⑤ Click the item you want to insert into the slide.

⑥ Click OK.

● The item is inserted into the slide in the specified slide layout.

⑦ Fill or format the item as desired.

TIPS

Try This!

You can create your own custom layouts if none of PowerPoint's built-in layouts give you exactly what you want. Click View, then click Slide Master to open the Slide Master view. In the Slide Master tab, click Insert Layout to create a new layout. Then click the Insert Placeholder menu and click the placeholder you want to add to the layout: Content, Text, Picture, and so on.

Reverse It!

After you switch to the new slide layout, you can move the placeholders around on the slide, adjust the formatting, and more. If you do not like the changes you have made, you can revert the slide to its original layout settings. Click Home and then click Reset.

Add emphasis by inserting a
CUSTOM BACKGROUND IMAGE

You can create a professional-looking and fully customized presentation by inserting a unique or custom background image into a slide. The background image, which can come from a digital camera, from a drawing program, or from a professional graphics design, can greatly enhance the look of your presentation.

An image inserted as a slide background does not print when the slides print. This is important, because if you apply a background image for its appearance, you do not want the image to conflict with the slide content. If you want the image to print with the slide, insert the image into the slide itself.

Background images are stretched or contracted to display on whatever screen that is being used. For example, a very small image, when the presentation is viewed in Slide Show Mode, automatically stretches to fit the screen. You will get better results if you use images that are approximately the same size as the monitor on which you will display them.

① Click the Design tab.

② Click Background Styles.

③ Click Format Background.

The Format Background dialog box appears.

④ Click the Picture or texture fill option (◉ changes to ◉).

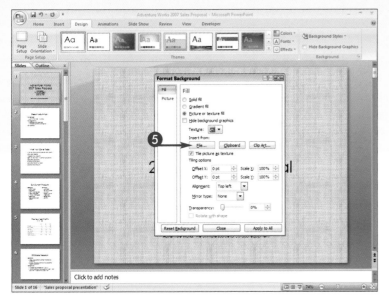

5 Click File.

The Insert Picture dialog box appears.

6 Click here and locate the folder containing the file you want to use as the background image.

7 Click the file you want to use.

8 Click Insert.

PowerPoint adds the background image to the slide.

Caution!
You will achieve the best results when you apply a background image that is 1-⅓ times wider than it is high. The width of most computer screen resolutions is 1-⅓ times the height, such as 1,024 pixels wide by 768 pixels high. Your background image should use these proportions as well. If the image you are using for a background is not in these proportions, the background image will look stretched or skewed when displayed.

Apply It!
You can also apply a texture to the slide backgrounds. To do so, follow Steps **1** to **4** above to activate the Picture or texture fill option. Click the Texture menu to display a gallery of textures. Click the texture you want to apply, and then click Apply to All.

Add emphasis by inserting a
CUSTOM BACKGROUND IMAGE

Pictures from digital cameras work well as background images for slides. Because most newer digital cameras create images with higher resolutions than are needed for use in presentations, you may want to reduce the size of the file in a graphics editing program before you use it for a background image.

In addition to images taken from a digital camera, you can use graphics files in any picture file format Microsoft Office supports, including BMP, JPEG, GIF, TIF, and PNG. Remember that if you use uncompressed files or files that are larger than

needed, you may unnecessarily increase the file size of your presentation or even slow its performance when delivering a slide show.

The best images to use for slide backgrounds are relatively uniform in color in the areas that contain text. For example, an image that is very light on one half and very dark on the other half would not work well as a background image because it is extremely difficult, if not impossible, to find a font and font color combination that work well against both light and dark backgrounds.

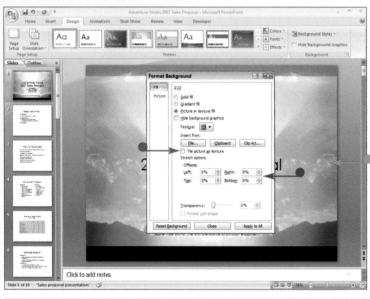

● PowerPoint applies the background image to the current slide.

● If the image is small, you can click Tile picture as texture to repeat the image so that it covers the entire slide background (◎ changes to ●).

● If the image does not quite cover the entire background, increase the values in the Left, Right, Top, and Bottom spin boxes as necessary to stretch the image to the full background size.

● If the image is dark or busy, you can make the slide text easier to read by increasing the Transparency value.

9 Click Apply to All.

Note: If you want the background to appear only on the current slide, skip to Step 10.

10 Click Close.

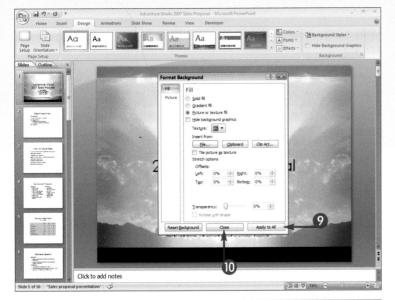

PowerPoint applies the background image to all the slides.

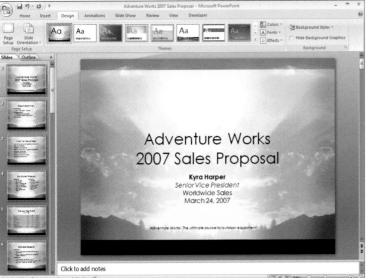

TIPS

Apply It!

To apply a background image to a Notes Master, click View, Master, and then Notes Master. In the Notes Master tab, click Background Styles and then follow Steps **4** to **10**. Use this option with caution because the notes text will print on top of the background image, which may affect legibility.

Try This!

Many templates come with images added to the Slide Master, and so those images appear on every slide. This is useful for displaying things like company logos or project icons. However, these images can also clash with your background image. If that happens, hide the Slide Master image. Select all of your slides, click the Design tab, and then click to activate the Hide Background Graphics check box.

Display Content in
DIFFERENT LANGUAGES

You can work with and edit content in any language supported by your Microsoft Windows operating system. The versions of Windows on which PowerPoint 2007 runs allow you to install support for most languages, including languages that are read from right to left and languages that require special keyboard mappings to produce characters that are not on standard U.S. English keyboards.

For example, if your Windows XP or Vista operating system is configured to support Japanese, PowerPoint 2007 can display Japanese text using Japanese characters, and can check for spelling errors using Japanese proofing tools.

When some languages are enabled, new features are uncovered. The most common features are proofing tools like the spell-checker. In addition, some languages enable new tools such as language-specific formatting options on the Format menu.

You can use the Microsoft Office 2007 Language Settings tool to enable language support in PowerPoint 2007. After the tool enables support for specific languages and you identify specific text in one of those languages, you can take advantage of language-specific tools.

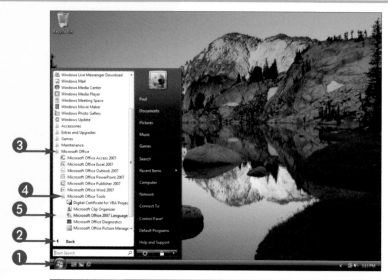

CONFIGURE OFFICE FOR MULTIPLE LANGUAGES

① Click the Start button.

② Click All Programs.

Note: When you click All Programs, the command changes to Back.

③ Click Microsoft Office.

④ Click Microsoft Office Tools.

⑤ Click Microsoft Office 2007 Language Settings.

The Microsoft Office Language Settings 2007 dialog box appears.

⑥ Scroll down and click the language you want to use.

⑦ Click the Add button to add languages to the Enabled editing languages section.

Repeat Steps **6** and **7** for each language you want to enable.

⑧ Click OK.

The next time you use PowerPoint, you can work with content in different languages.

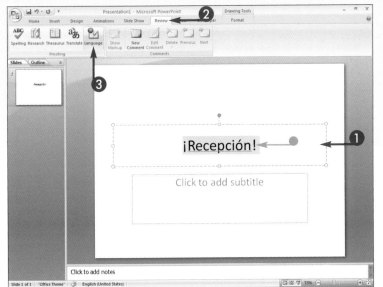

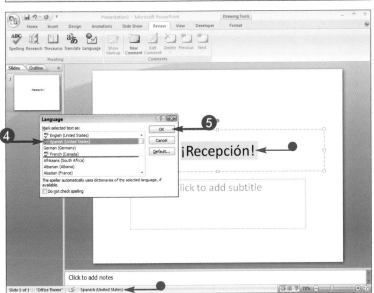

DIFFICULTY LEVEL

① Click and drag to highlight the text that you want to mark as a particular language.

● PowerPoint has marked this text as a spelling error because it is treating the text as English.

② Click the Review tab.

③ Click Language.

The Language dialog box appears.

④ Scroll down and click the language in which you want the selected text to appear.

⑤ Click OK.

● The language of the selected text is changed.

Tools enabled by that language are now available for use.

● PowerPoint no longer marks the text as a spelling error.

TIPS

Did You Know?

You can mark all text for a specific language by first clicking the Home tab, then Select, and then Select All. (You can also press Ctrl+A.) Now follow Steps **1** to **5** in the Identify Text as a Specific Language section above.

Caution!

Microsoft Windows system requirements differ for each language you want to use. For example, some languages that are read from right to left and some of the Asian languages have specific system requirements that must be met before you can type in those languages. However, you can open and display content in presentations that were created in any language in which Office has been enabled by using the Microsoft Office Language Settings 2007 tool.

Create a
CUSTOM SLIDE THEME

You can create a custom slide theme that applies your own colors, fonts, and effects to a presentation.

The look of a PowerPoint presentation is governed by the applied *theme*, which is a collection of formatting options that specify the presentation colors, fonts, and effects.

PowerPoint comes with several built-in color schemes that cover a dozen different slide elements, including text, the slide background, hypertext links, and accents such as chart data markers. You can also create custom color schemes.

PowerPoint comes with several built-in font schemes, each of which specifies one font for slide headings

(titles) and another for the slide body (regular text such as bullets). As with colors, you can also create custom font schemes.

The effects govern graphical elements such as 3-D, glowing edges, and shadows.

PowerPoint comes with 20 built-in themes that you can apply to the slides in your presentation. If none of the built-in themes are suitable, you can create your own custom theme that includes custom colors, fonts, and effects. You can save this theme and apply it to any presentation.

DEFINE A CUSTOM SLIDE THEME

1. Click the Design tab.

2. Click Colors and select a set of colors for the custom theme.

3. Click Fonts and select a set of fonts for the custom theme.

4. Click Effects and select a set of effects for the custom theme.

5. Click here.

The Themes gallery appears.

6. Click Save Current Theme.

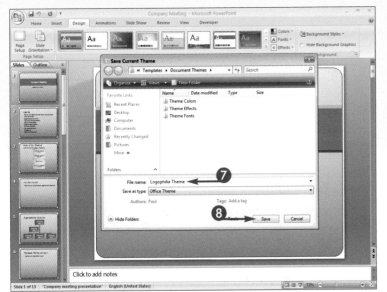

The Save Current Theme dialog box appears.

⑦ Type a name to assign a unique name for your theme.

⑧ Click Save.

PowerPoint saves the theme.

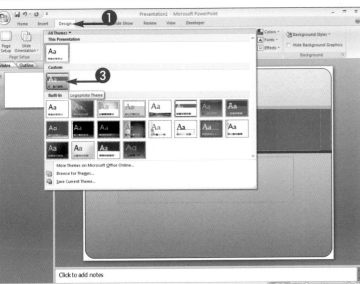

APPLY A CUSTOM COLOR SCHEME

① Click the Design tab.

② In the Themes group, click the Themes gallery's down arrow.

③ Click the custom slide theme.

PowerPoint applies the custom theme to the current presentation.

TIPS

More Options!

When you click a theme in the Themes gallery, PowerPoint applies the theme colors, fonts, and effects to every slide in the current presentation. If you want to apply the theme to only some of the slides in the presentation, first select those slides, display the Themes gallery, right-click the theme you want to use, and then click Apply to Selected Slides.

Remove It!

All the custom themes you create appear in the Themes gallery in the Custom section. If you created a theme that you no longer use, you should delete it to reduce the clutter in the Custom section. Click Design and then click the More button in the Themes group. In the Themes gallery, right-click the custom theme you want to remove and then click Delete. When PowerPoint asks you to confirm the deletion, click Yes.

Chapter 3

Add Impact with Graphics

You can enhance the effectiveness of your presentations when you use graphics to help communicate your message. For example, PowerPoint 2007's new SmartArt graphics can help you display complex data in an easy to understand visual format. Similarly, you can put content from your scanner to work for you by inserting photos, drawings, and documents into your presentations. For example, if you have a printed photograph you would like to include on a slide, PowerPoint communicates directly with your scanner to scan the photograph and then insert it into your presentation.

After your images or graphics are in your presentations, you can learn how to add effects to get them noticed. You can add colorful borders to make the images stand out, and you can crop photos so that only the most important parts are included in your slides.

If you have ever wondered how to make an image with a white background blend in on a slide with a color background, you can use the Set Transparent Color tool to make it work. You can also add clarity to your presentation by adding text to AutoShapes or enhancing AutoShapes with three-dimensional effects. You can even learn how to compress graphics to manage the size of presentations and make them load more quickly.

You can create a Photo Album that displays a collection of images or photographs in one of many available styles. Photo Album presentations are professionally formatted and save you time because, after selecting which images to include, all of the work of preparing the presentation is done for you.

Top 100

Communicate Information with a
SMARTART GRAPHIC

You can illustrate concepts and convey complex information in a visual form by using the new SmartArt feature. The SmartArt format is based on the XML (eXtensible Markup Language) standard. A SmartArt graphic combines text, predefined shapes, and in some cases arrows and images into a diagram. SmartArt illustrates concepts in seven categories: List, Process, Cycle, Hierarchy, Relationship, Matrix, and Pyramid.

Lists illustrate concepts that are sequential or that form a progression or group. The Process category covers concepts that progress from one stage to another, where the overall progress has a beginning

and an end. Cycle concepts progress from one stage to another in a repeating pattern. The Hierarchy category shows the relative importance of one thing over another, or to show how one thing is contained within another.

The Relationship category covers concepts that show how two or more items are related. You use a Matrix graphic to show the relationship between the entirety of something and its components, organized as quadrants. Finally, the Pyramid category covers concepts with components that are proportional to each other or interconnected in some way.

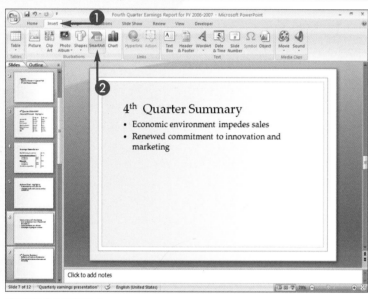

1 Click the Insert tab.

2 Click SmartArt.

The Choose a SmartArt Graphic dialog box appears.

3 Click a category.

4 Click the SmartArt graphic you want to insert.

5 Click OK.

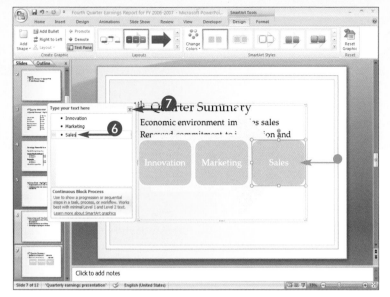

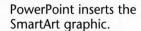

PowerPoint inserts the SmartArt graphic.

6 Use the Text Pane to type the text for each item you want to include in the SmartArt graphic.

● PowerPoint adds the text to the SmartArt graphic.

7 Click the Close button.

PowerPoint closes the Text Pane.

<!---->
DIFFICULTY LEVEL

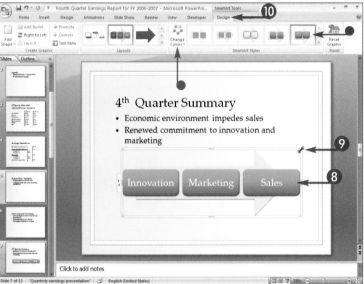

8 Click the border of the SmartArt graphic.

When you click the image, the image resizing handles become visible.

9 Click and drag any corner of the image diagonally toward the opposite corner of the image to resize the graphic.

10 Click the Design tab.

● You can click Change Colors and then click the color you want.

● You can click a style in the SmartArt Styles gallery.

TIPS

More Options!

PowerPoint populates each SmartArt graphic with just a few shapes into which you can add text. If you need more shapes, click an existing shape, click the Design tab, and then click the Add Shape menu. Click either Add Shape After or Add Shape Before. Click Text Pane and then type your text for the new shape.

More Options!

To format a SmartArt shape, click the shape and then click the Format tab. Click Change Shape to select a different shape. Click Larger or Smaller to change the size of the shape. Use the Shape Styles gallery to apply options for the shape fill, outline, and effects. Alternatively, apply your own options using the Shape Fill, Shape Outline, and Shape Effects lists.

ADD CONNECTOR LINES
to objects

If you use shapes, text boxes, or other objects on a slide, you can make that slide easier to read by adding connector lines that connect the slide objects. *Connector lines* are lines that PowerPoint automatically draws for you between two objects. For example, if you want the user to read Object A first and then Object B, you can add a connector line between them, where the line includes an arrow that leads the reader from Object A to Object B.

Connector lines allow you to establish links between various objects on a slide. If you have ever seen or worked with flowcharts, then you already have a good idea of what connector lines do because flowchart elements have lines that lead from one element to another. You can use connector lines to create your own version of a flowchart or diagram.

Connector lines come in several different styles. After you add a connector line between two slide objects, you can move either or both objects, and the connector line resizes to maintain the connection between them.

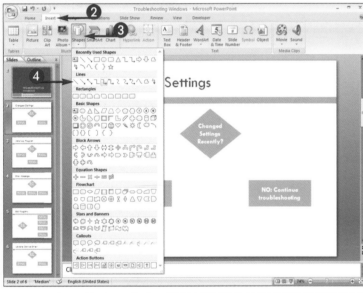

① Display the slide containing the two objects you want to connect.

② Click the Insert tab.

③ Click Shapes.

The Shapes gallery appears.

④ Click the connector style you want to apply.

⑤ Position the mouse pointer over the first item.

● Red connector handles surround the object.

⑥ Click the handle you want to use as the anchor point.

PowerPoint establishes the handle you click as the first anchor point.

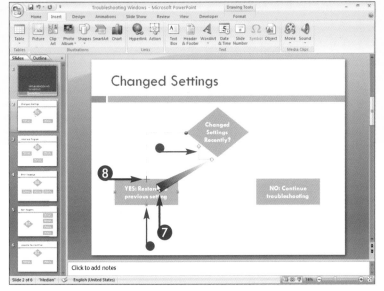

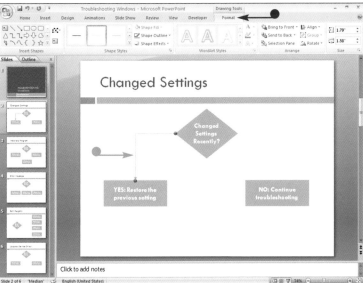

- PowerPoint adds the basic connector shape to the slide.

7 Drag the other end of the connector over the object to which you want to connect.

A dashed line trails your connector line as you drag to the other object on the slide.

- Red connector handles surround the object.

8 Click the handle you want to use as the second anchor point.

- PowerPoint draws a connector line between the two objects.

- You can click Format and apply formatting to the connector line using the drawing tools.

22

DIFFICULTY LEVEL

TIPS

More Options!

If you do not like the connector type you chose, you can change it to a Straight Connector, an Elbow Connector, or a Curved Connector. Right-click the connector line, click Connector Type, and then click the type you prefer.

Did You Know?

If you prefer the look of the Shape feature's Block Arrows, which have a chunkier style and can curve, you can use them to simulate connectors. However, you establish the connections between two objects by drawing the shapes yourself. No blue connector handles appear to assist you, and if you move a slide object, the Block Arrow shape does not resize to maintain the connection between the items.

Emphasize images with
BORDERS

You can make images in your presentations stand out when you add image borders. For example, in a presentation where the slide background color is similar to the colors used on an image on the slide, add a colorful image border to make the slide stand out against the background.

You can use image borders to highlight items that users can click for some other effect. Traditionally, items you can click on a Web site have a colorful highlighted border around them. If you add a

hyperlink to an image in PowerPoint, borders are not added automatically. You can add borders manually to images that use effects like hyperlinks. For more information about adding hyperlinks to images, see Tasks #61 and #62.

Image borders in PowerPoint are simply lines placed around images. The true power in image borders is the ability to use virtually any color or any line width to make your image borders truly unique.

① Right-click the image.

② Click Format Picture.

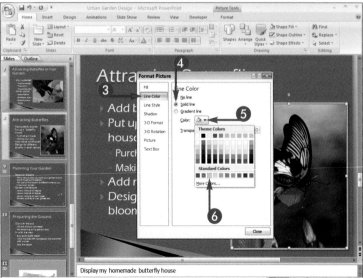

The Format Picture dialog box appears.

③ Click Line Color.

④ Click the Solid line option (◎ changes to ⦿).

⑤ Click the Color menu button.

⑥ Click the color you want to use for the border.

⑦ Click Line Style.

⑧ Use the Width spin box to set the width of the border.

⑨ Click Close.

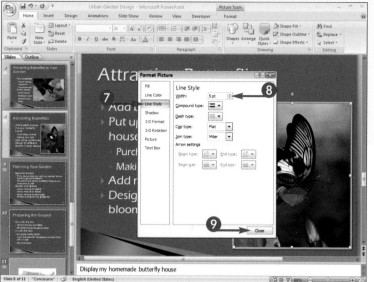

PowerPoint updates the image with the new border.

TIPS

Did You Know?

Line widths are measured in points. A point is equivalent to $\frac{1}{72}$ of an inch. A line that is 12 points high is 12 dots high, or the height of a capital letter I in a 12-point font.

More Options!

You can also use dashed or dotted lines for your borders. Follow Steps **1** to **7** above, click the Dash type menu, and then click the dashed or dotted line you want to use.

Try This!

You can make your images stand out even more by adding a drop shadow. Follow Steps **1** and **2**, click Shadow, and then click a shadow type from the Presets menu.

CROP IMAGES
to attract attention

You can attract attention to just the part of pictures or graphics that you want when you crop an image. You can think of cropping an image as similar to cutting the edges off a photograph or even cutting off unnecessary or unwanted parts of a photograph before you place it in a photo album. Cropping in PowerPoint is similar in that you remove the portions outside the area on which you want to focus. This helps you not only to fit a large image into a slide, but also to attract the viewer's attention to the most important part of the image.

Cropping is especially useful if you routinely add digital camera images to slides. Digital images are often sized at a ratio of 1:1.5. For example, an image that is 4 inches high will be 6 inches wide, or 4 x 6 inches. If you want to display the image as a square, you can crop to reduce the width. You can crop almost any type of image, except for animated GIF files.

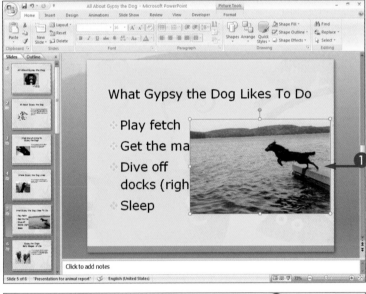

① Click the image you want to crop.

The Picture Tools "tab" and the Format tab appear.

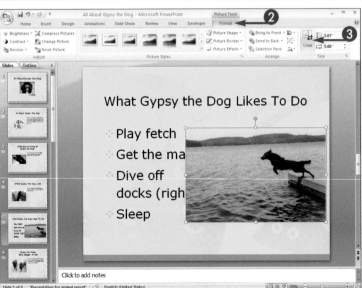

② Click the Format tab.

③ Click Crop.

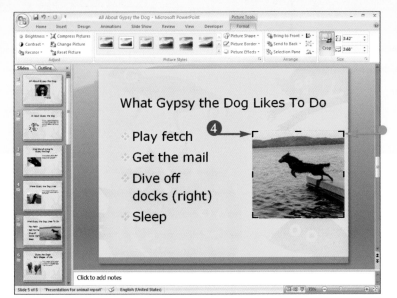

- Cropping handles appear around the picture.

④ Click one of the cropping handles, and then drag toward the center of the picture.

Repeat Step **4** for each side or corner you want to crop.

DIFFICULTY LEVEL

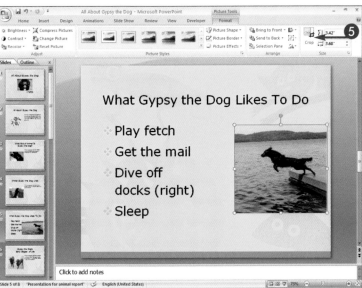

⑤ Click the Crop button on the Picture toolbar.

PowerPoint crops the image.

TIPS

Did You Know?

After you crop an image it will appear smaller, but it will not take up less space in your presentation until you compress it. To learn more about compressing images, see Task #25.

Apply It!

After you crop an image, you can reposition it on the screen if you want. Follow Steps **1** to **5** above, and then click and drag the image to the desired location.

Reverse It!

If you crop the picture incorrectly, or if you change your mind about cropping the picture, you can restore the image. Click the image, click the Format tab, and then click Reset Picture.

COMPRESS GRAPHICS
to make presentations load faster

You can compress graphics from within PowerPoint to minimize the size of graphics files. Compressing graphics files is a good idea because the smaller you make your presentation files, the faster those presentations download and open.

Graphics should be compressed after they are manipulated in PowerPoint. For example, if you scan an image into a presentation, it is likely to be a high-quality file suitable for print, but may include more richness than can be displayed on standard monitors or projectors. If your presentation is likely to be viewed on monitors rather than printed, you can compress the images for Web or screen resolution.

Even if you expect to print your presentations with high quality, you should compress graphics if they have been resized or cropped. When you resize or crop images, the visual image of the graphics file changes, but the actual size of the file remains unchanged. The Compress Pictures tool removes cropped or resized portions of images from files and decreases the file size.

Before performing this task, make sure that a graphics specialist working with your department or company has not already compressed the available images in advance.

① Click the picture you want to compress.

② Click the Format tab.

③ Click Compress Pictures.

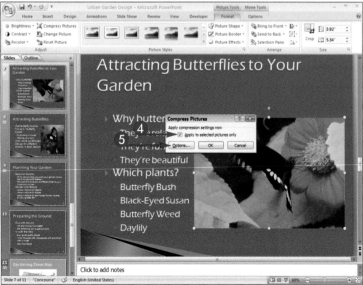

The Compress Pictures dialog box appears.

④ Click Apply to selected pictures only (☐ changes to ☑) to compress only the picture you selected.

⑤ Click Options.

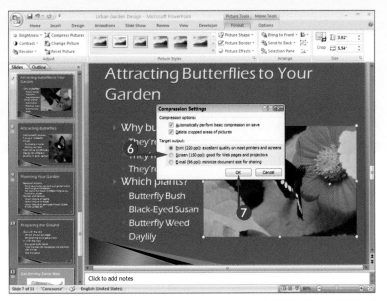

The Compression Settings dialog box appears.

⑥ Click a resolution (◎ changes to ◉).

⑦ Click OK.

⑧ Click OK.

PowerPoint compresses the image.

Did You Know?

You can control how much compression PowerPoint applies by using the following Target Output options in the Compression Settings dialog box:

● **Print (220 ppi).** Click this option to maintain picture quality by using the least compression.

● **Screen (150 ppi).** Click this option if you will be sharing the presentation on the Web or over a network.

● **E-mail (96 ppi).** Click this option if you will be sharing the presentation via e-mail.

Caution!

You can compress all the pictures in your presentation at once. Follow the steps above, but skip Step **4** to leave the Apply to selected pictures only check box deactivated. Use caution, though. This setting means that PowerPoint will apply the compression options to all the pictures in your presentation.

Display pictures in a
PHOTO ALBUM

You can quickly create a photo album presentation to display images or graphics in a variety of styles. The Photo Album tool creates a brand-new presentation with the photos and graphics you select arranged on each slide. The images you choose can be in any file format PowerPoint supports, and it is not necessary for the files to be located in the same directory.

The Photo Album tool saves time because it allows you to insert many images at once and then formats the slides with the selected number of pictures. For

example, without the Photo Album tool, if you wanted to arrange six images on two slides, you would have to create the slides, insert the images into the presentation, and then resize and reposition the images on the two slides. The Photo Album tool performs these tasks for you and applies selected special effects to the images, such as corner tabs or special shapes.

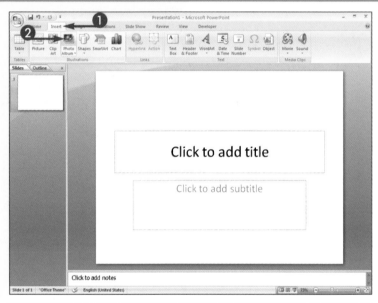

① Click the Insert tab.

② Click the top portion of the Photo Album button.

The Photo Album dialog box appears.

③ Click File/Disk.

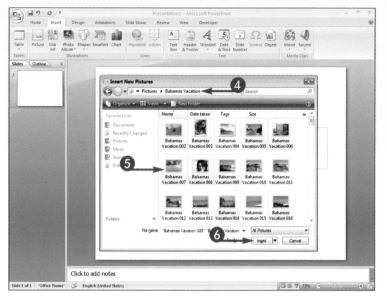

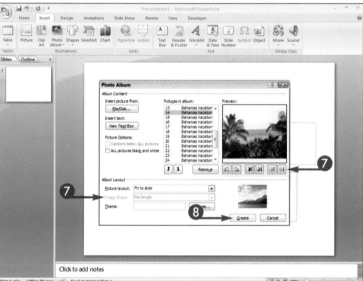

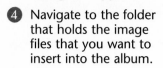

The Insert New Pictures dialog box appears.

④ Navigate to the folder that holds the image files that you want to insert into the album.

⑤ Select the picture files to insert.

Note: You can Shift-click or Ctrl-click to select multiple image files in the list.

⑥ Click Insert.

The Photo Album dialog box now lists the photos you chose.

⑦ Adjust the photo album by choosing the desired settings.

⑧ Click Create.

PowerPoint creates the photo album presentation with Photo Album as the title. PowerPoint creates a plain white title slide for you and adds your images to subsequent slides in the presentation.

Note: Save and name your photo album presentation.

More Options!

In the Photo Album dialog box, use the Rotate buttons to rotate the current image into the correct position; use the Contrast buttons to increase or reduce the contrast of the current image; and use the Brightness buttons to increase or decrease the brightness of the current image.

Did You Know?

A photo album is not all that different from a slide show. You can apply a theme or other formatting to the photo album, insert additional slides as needed, run the photo album presentation as an on-screen slide show, and more. The key difference is that you can use the Photo Album or Edit Photo Album dialog boxes to set up a picture layout or frame all the slides. You also can use the dialog box to reorder the pictures or make changes to picture settings such as rotation.

BLEND GRAPHICS
into the background

You can make parts of a graphic transparent against a colored background by using the Set Transparent Color option. The Set Transparent Color option is helpful if you are placing an image or logo onto a slide that is not rectangular and has a background color different from the background color used in your slide. Images that do not have irregular edges, such as rectangles, are not usually good candidates for using the Transparency option because rectangular images are easily cropped, while images with irregular or angular edges are difficult to crop.

See Task #24 for more information about cropping.

The Set Transparent Color option works when you click in an area of the image that contains the single color that you want to become transparent. After you click the color that you want to make transparent, every instance of that color in the image is made transparent, allowing the background color or image to show through. The Set Transparent Color option can be used with most images PowerPoint supports except for animated GIF files.

1 Click the image you want to work with.

2 Click the Format tab.

3 Click Recolor.

4 Click Set Transparent Color.

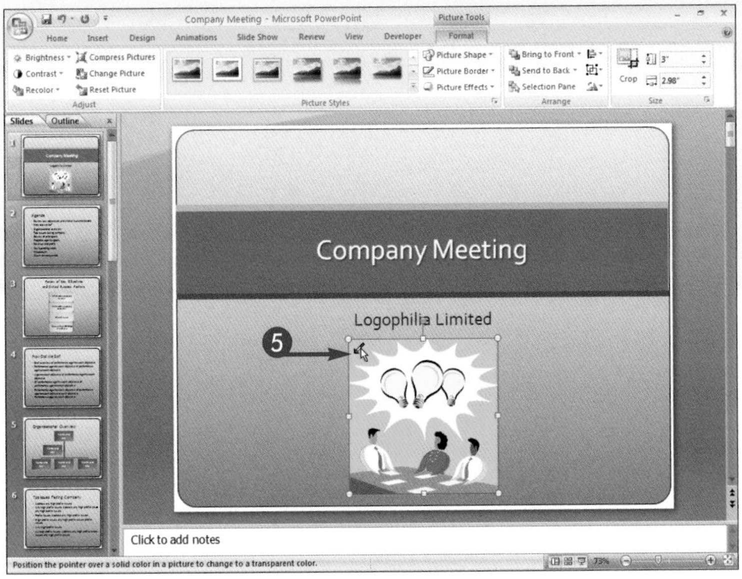

changes to .

5. In the image, click the color that you want to make transparent.

#27

DIFFICULTY LEVEL

PowerPoint makes the color transparent.

TIPS

Attention!

Many images, especially photographs, appear to have a uniform background color, when in reality there are slight variations in color. When the Set Transparent Color option is used on these images, not all of the background is made transparent.

Caution!

The Set Transparent Color option makes all instances of the selected color transparent. If that color is included in the main part of the graphic, it will also be made transparent.

Did You Know?

If you do not get the desired results with the Set Transparent Color option, you can use a graphic editing program to create transparent GIF images. These images already have areas defined to be transparent, so you will not need to use the Set Transparent Color option.

ADD TEXT
to your shapes

You can insert text into most shapes to convey important messages more clearly. Shapes make it easy to add arrows, stars, banners, callout boxes, and more to slides. Without text in the shapes, however, a user viewing your presentation online or in printed format might not understand the point of a shape. For example, an arrow shape may focus attention on an important part of a chart or graph, but without text on the arrow, the user might have a difficult time understanding why it is important.

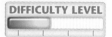

Did You Know?

Shapes carry the most impact when the design of the shape conveys an important message. If the text itself is much more important than the design of the shape, consider adding WordArt, which adds highly formatted text to slides, rather than a shape.

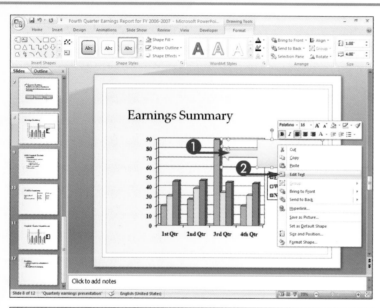

① Right-click the shape to which you want to add text.

The Edit menu appears.

② Click Edit Text.

An insertion point is added to the graphic.

③ Type the desired text.

④ Click outside of the shape.

APPLY 3-D EFFECTS
to make graphics stand out

DIFFICULTY LEVEL

You can add 3-D effects to shapes and other graphics to make them appear three-dimensional by using the 3-D Rotation gallery on the Drawing Tools Format tab. Three-dimensional effects make graphics more attention-getting because they add depth and an additional layer of color to slides.

3-D effects add shadows to graphics to help make them look truly three-dimensional. 3-D effects automatically use the coloring scheme that is used on the slide on which the graphic appears so that the effects are coordinated with other slide content.

Try This!

For a more subtle effect, you can add a drop shadow to any graphic. Drop shadows add dimension to images and other graphics files. Click the image, click Format, click Shape Effects (or Picture Effects), click Shadow, and then click the shadow style you want.

① Click the shape to which you want to add a 3-D effect.

② Click the Format tab.

③ Click Shape Effects.

Note: If you're working with a picture, click Picture Effects, instead.

④ Click 3-D Rotation.

The 3-D Rotation gallery appears.

⑤ Click the 3-D rotation effect you want to use.

● PowerPoint applies the 3-D effect to the image.

ALIGN GRAPHICS PERFECTLY
using the grid and guidelines

PowerPoint offers two features — the grid and guidelines — that help you position objects and placeholders more precisely and evenly, which enhances the overall look of your slides.

There are many elements that go into a professional-looking presentation. One of the little things that differentiates a solid presentation design from an amateur one is the proper alignment of objects on each slide. For example, if you have two or three clip art images running along the bottom of a slide, this

arrangement looks best when the bottom edges of each image are aligned. To help out, you can use the grid, which appears like graph paper lines on your slide.

PowerPoint also offers the drawing guides, which are dashed lines — one vertical and one horizontal — that appear over the slide area. When you click and drag an object near one of these guide lines, PowerPoint snaps the object to the line, so aligning objects is quick and easy.

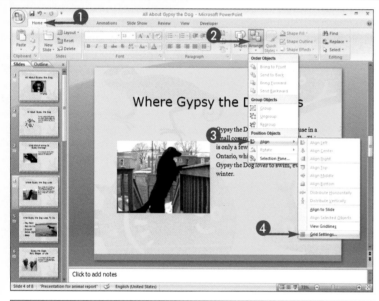

① Click the Home tab.

② Click Arrange.

③ Click Align.

④ Click Grid Settings.

The Grid and Guides dialog box appears.

⑤ Click to activate the Display grid on screen check box (☐ changes to ☑).

⑥ Click to activate the Display drawing guides on screen check box (☐ changes to ☑).

⑦ Click OK.

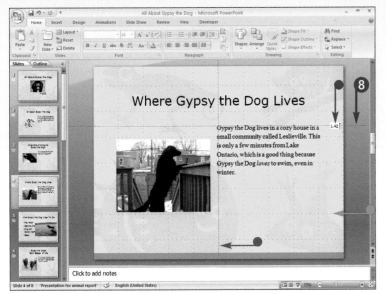

30

- The grid appears as dotted lines.
- The guidelines appear as dashed lines.

8 Drag a guideline.

- A value representing the new position of the guide appears as you drag.

DIFFICULTY LEVEL

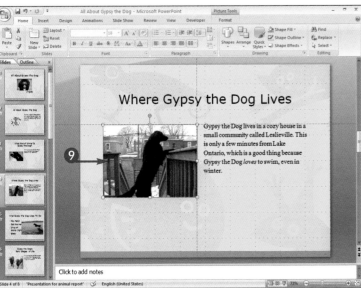

9 Select and drag an object to line it up with the grid or guide.

TIPS

More Options!

PowerPoint also offers the Snap To feature that enables you to automatically line up objects along grid lines. Follow Steps **1** to **4** to open the Grid and Guides dialog box. Click to activate the Snap objects to grid check box, if needed, and then click OK. Now when you move an object around the slide, if it is close to a grid line, it automatically snaps to align with the grid.

Remove It!

When you are done with the grid and guidelines, repeat Steps **1** to **7** to hide them.

Did You Know?

You can also toggle the gridlines on and off by clicking the Home tab, Arrange, Align, and then View Gridlines. Alternatively, click the View tab and then click the Gridlines check box.

Using Timesaving Tools

You can accomplish work faster in PowerPoint with tools that can help make routine work less tedious. For example, if you have slides in another presentation that would fit with your current presentation, you can paste those slides into your current work without having to recreate the slides. You can also get a quick start on your work by converting a Word outline into a PowerPoint presentation.

You can eliminate guesswork by using the Format Painter to copy text and graphics effects from one place to another in your presentation. You can even turn one of your favorite presentations into a Design Template that you can use to create future presentations.

If you have access to a SharePoint site where you work, you can take advantage of one of PowerPoint 2007's most useful features: the Slide Library. This is a slide repository that resides on a server. You can use slides from a slide library and publish your own slides to a slide library.

If you have ever wondered if there is a faster way to perform repetitive tasks, macros can help. You can create macros that help automate tasks by using PowerPoint's built-in support for Visual Basic for Applications code.

Top 100

PASTE SLIDES
from one presentation to another

You can easily copy and then paste slides from one presentation to another. Slides you copy are placed onto the Office Clipboard where they are stored until you either collect 24 more items or clear items from the Office Clipboard. This allows you to copy slides, text, and graphics from a variety of presentations first, and then selectively paste them when you are ready. If you choose not to use the Office Clipboard, you can paste the slides as long as they were the last item copied or cut.

The Slide Sorter View and the slide tab on the Normal View are the most convenient places to copy slides because the thumbnail images enable you to select and then copy more than one slide at a time. When you copy slides from one presentation to another, by default, the copied slides take on the theme of the new presentation. You can also choose to maintain the existing format of the copied slides.

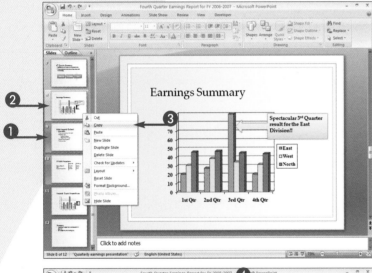

① Click to select the slides you want to copy.

   Note: You can press Ctrl-click to select more than one slide.

② Right-click any selected slide.

③ Click Copy.

④ Click the View tab.

⑤ Click Switch Windows.

⑥ Click the presentation to which you want to copy the slides.

70

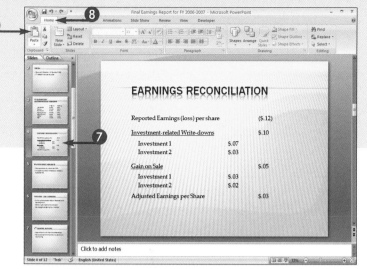

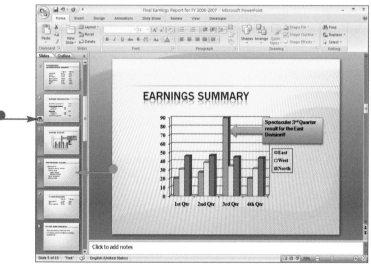

31

The presentation where you want to insert the slides appears.

⑦ Click where you want to insert the slides.

⑧ Click the Home tab.

⑨ Click the top half of the Paste button.

You can also press Ctrl+V to paste the slides.

● PowerPoint pastes the slides into the presentation.

● The Paste Options Smart Tag appears.

If you want to revert the pasted slides to their original format, click the Paste Options button and then click the Keep Source Formatting option.

TIPS

Did You Know?

You can also paste slides from the Office Clipboard. Click Home and then click the dialog launcher button in the lower right corner of the Clipboard group. In the current presentation, use the Slide Sorter or Slide tab in Normal View to click where you would like to insert the slides. In the Office Clipboard, click the slide you want to paste.

Apply It!

You can selectively copy more than one slide at a time by viewing slides in the Slide tab in Normal View, and then Ctrl+clicking for each slide you want to select. When you finish selecting slides, press Ctrl+C to copy them.

TURN A WORD OUTLINE
into a PowerPoint Presentation

You can turn an existing Word outline into a slide show in PowerPoint.

Given the hierarchical structure of a PowerPoint outline, you may not be surprised to hear that you can convert Word's own outline hierarchy — the styles Heading 1, Heading 2, and so on — into a PowerPoint outline.

PowerPoint interprets a Heading 1 style as a top-level item in a presentation outline. In other words, each time PowerPoint comes across Heading 1 text, it starts a new slide and the text associated with the Heading 1 style becomes the title of the slide.

PowerPoint interprets a Heading 2 style as a second-level item in a presentation outline. So each paragraph of Heading 2 text becomes a main bullet (or subtitle) in the presentation.

Finally, PowerPoint interprets the styles Heading 3, Heading 4, and so on as lower-level items in the presentation outline.

Note that when PowerPoint creates the new presentation from the Word outline, it does not assign slide designs or layouts. It is up to you to add formatting and slide designs, and to illustrate the slides with any graphic items, such as clip art, shapes, or photos.

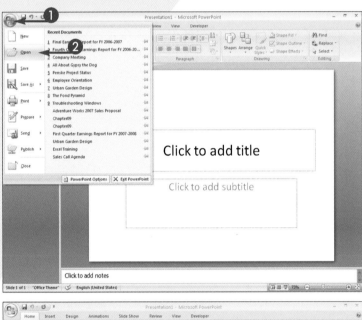

① Click the Office button.

② Click Open.

The keyboard shortcut for displaying the Open dialog box is Ctrl+O.

The Open dialog box appears.

③ Use this list to click All Outlines.

④ Navigate to the folder that contains the outline.

⑤ Click the Word document you want to convert into a presentation.

⑥ Click Open.

PowerPoint converts the content of the file into a presentation and lists each slide in the Slides pane.

TIPS

Did You Know?

Another method you can use is to start a new presentation and then display the Outline pane. Click Home, click the bottom half of the New Slide button, and then click Slides from Outline. In the Insert Outline dialog box, click the Word file and then click Insert.

Caution!

Unfortunately, PowerPoint does not enable you to work on the outline in Word and import it into PowerPoint at the same time. PowerPoint displays an error message if the Word document you are trying to convert is already open elsewhere. Therefore, be sure to close the Word document before attempting to import the outline.

COPY FORMATTING
from one slide to another

You can easily transfer formatting from one area of text to another with the Format Painter. The Format Painter allows you to click one piece of text, copy the formatting of that text, and then apply that formatting to another piece of text. The Format Painter does not copy the text, just the formatting of the text.

The Format Painter is especially useful when you open a presentation that you did not create and you do not know what fonts, font styles, and other formatting were used when it was created. For example, if some text in your presentation uses a custom color and a font that is unfamiliar to you, you can save time by simply using the Format Painter to copy the formatting and apply it to your presentation. Without the Format Painter, you would have to look up the RGB value of the color used, look up the formatting used, and then manually apply the color and the special formatting to the text.

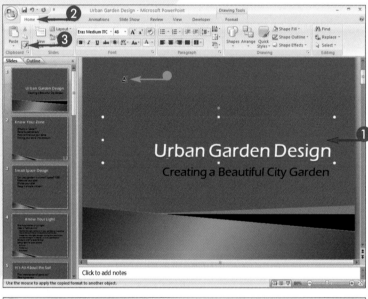

① Click the text from which you want to copy the format.

② Click the Home tab.

③ Double-click the Format Painter button.

● The ⬚ changes to the ⬚.

④ Switch to the slide that contains the text to which you want to apply the copied format.

⑤ Click the object that contains the text you want to work with.

6 Click and drag to highlight the text to which you want to apply the copied format.

#33

● PowerPoint applies the formatting of the original text to the selected text.

7 Click the Home tab.

8 Click Format Painter.

The changes back to ⌖ .

TIPS

More Options!

You can also use the Format Painter when you have a Shape in your presentation that has been formatted with colors, shadows, gradients, and other effects that could be difficult to identify and then reproduce on another Shape or image. You can follow the steps above to copy formatting from one image or Shape to another.

Did You Know?

When you double-click the Format Painter button, PowerPoint leaves the button activated after you apply the formatting to some text. If you want to apply the formatting to other text, repeat Steps **4** to **6** as often as necessary. When you are done, follow Steps **7** and **8** to deactivate the Format Painter button.

PUBLISH SLIDES
to a Slide Library

You can make slides available to other people on your network by publishing those slides to a slide library. Earlier this chapter explained how to paste slides from one presentation to another (see task #31). However, that technique works only for your own slides or for network users who have permission to access your presentations. In many business situations, it's better to make particular slides available to a wider group of people. For example, if your company requires a standard opening slide or a slide with a legal disclaimer, it's best to have the

most up-to-date versions of such slides available to a wide group of people.

Similarly, you may work with a department or with a project team, and the members of that department or team may require access to common slides.

For these kinds of situations, if your company runs SharePoint Server 2007, you can take advantage of *slide libraries* that contain individual slides. Users who can access the SharePoint site can reuse those slides in their presentations. First, however, you must publish one or more slides to a slide library.

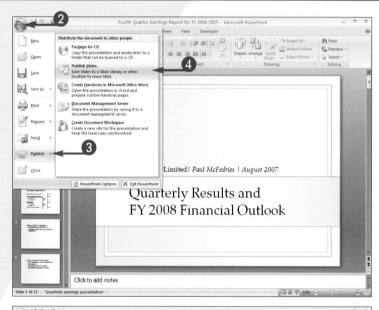

① Open the presentation that contains the slide or slides you want to publish.

② Click the Office button.

③ Click Publish.

④ Click Publish Slides.

The Publish Slides dialog box appears.

⑤ Click to activate the check box for each slide you want to publish (☐ changes to ☑).

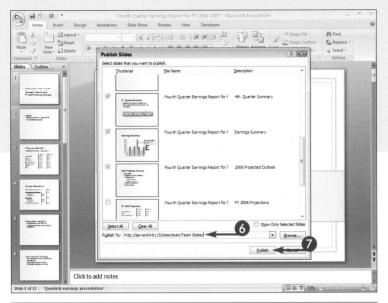

⑥ Use the Publish To text box to type the address of the slide library on the SharePoint site.

⑦ Click Publish.

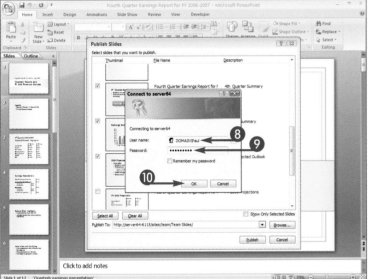

If your SharePoint site requires that you log in, you see the Connect dialog box.

⑧ Type your SharePoint site user name.

⑨ Type your password.

⑩ Click OK.

PowerPoint publishes the selected slides to the slide library.

Attention!

You cannot publish a slide to a slide library if no library exists on the SharePoint site. Ask your SharePoint administrator to create a library. If you have Contribute privileges on the site, you can do it yourself. Log in to the SharePoint site, click Site Settings, and then click Create. On the Create page under the Libraries heading, click Slide Library. Type a Name and optional Description, and then click Create.

Did You Know?

You can also publish slides from within the slide library itself. Log in to the SharePoint site, open the slide library, click Upload, and then click Publish Slides. In the Browse dialog box, click the presentation you want to use and then click Open to display the Publish Slides dialog box. Follow Steps **5** to **10** in this task to publish the slides.

REUSE SLIDES
from a Slide Library

You can save time, be more consistent, and ensure accuracy by selecting a slide located in a slide library and using it in one of your presentations.

After you or other members of your department or team have published some slides to a slide library, those slides become available for reuse in presentations. This can be a real timesaver because if someone else has already done the work to create a slide you need, you can add it to your presentation in just a few seconds, which is much faster than recreating the slide from scratch.

Reusing a slide from a slide library also ensures consistency among the members of a department or team. If each member uses the same slide for common topics, presentations from different members will have a consistent look and feel, which enhances the professionalism of all the presentations.

Reusing slides from a slide library also ensures that you are using the most up-to-date version of the slide. PowerPoint can automatically check published slides for changes and alert you when a new version is available.

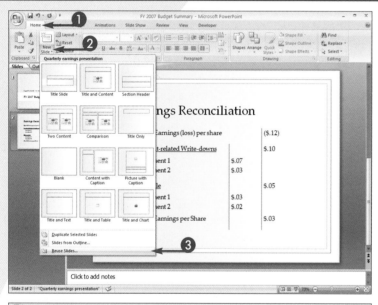

① Click the Home tab.

② Click the bottom half of the New Slide button.

③ Click Reuse Slides.

The Reuse Slides task pane appears.

④ Type the address of the slide library you want to use.

⑤ Click the Go button.

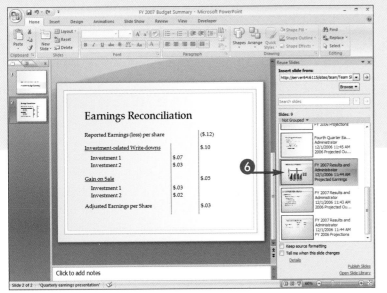

Thumbnail versions of the slides in the slide library appear.

Note: If you want to get a closer look at a slide, position the mouse pointer over the slide to see a magnified view.

⑥ Click the slide you want to reuse.

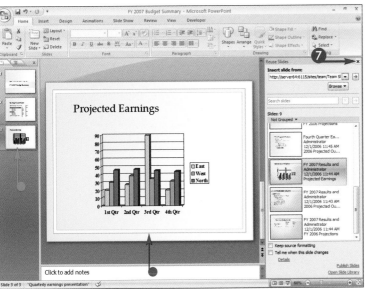

● PowerPoint downloads the slide and inserts it at the end of the presentation.

● PowerPoint formats the slide with the current presentation's theme.

⑦ Click the Close button.

PowerPoint closes the Reuse Slides task pane.

TIPS

Important!

Other people can work on slides in a slide library, and someone in your team might upload a more recent version. To allow for this, click to activate the Tell me when this slide changes check box before you click the slide. To check for an updated version of the slide, right-click the slide in the Slides tab, click Check for Updates, and then click Check This Slide for Changes.

More Options!

If there are many slides in the library, you can make it easier to find the one you want by grouping the slides. In the Reuse Slides pane, click Not Grouped and then click a grouping option: Group by presentation title, Group by editor, or Group by date modified.

SEND SLIDES
from a Slide Library to PowerPoint

If you have access to a SharePoint slide library, you can send one or more slides from that library to a new or existing PowerPoint presentation.

Task #36 explained how to use the Reuse Slides command to display the contents of a SharePoint slide library in PowerPoint, and then add one or more slides from that library to an open presentation. This works well for small slide libraries, but if you have access to a large library, you may find that the Reuse Slides pane is too small and cramped to show the slides properly and work with them efficiently.

A better solution is to log on to the SharePoint site and work with the slide library directly. The larger interface enables you to see more slides, get a better view of the slide properties — including the slide's name and description — and even edit those properties. Best of all, you can also easily select one or more slides that you want to use in a presentation, and then copy the slides to PowerPoint. You can copy them to a new presentation or to any open presentation.

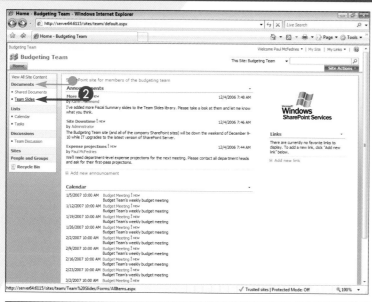

① Log on to the SharePoint site.

② Click the link to the slide library.

● If you do not see a direct link to the slide library, click Documents and then click the slide library.

The slide library appears.

③ Click to activate the check box beside each slide you want to send to PowerPoint (☐ changes to ☑).

● To see a larger version of a slide, click the slide thumbnail.

④ Click Copy Slide to Presentation.

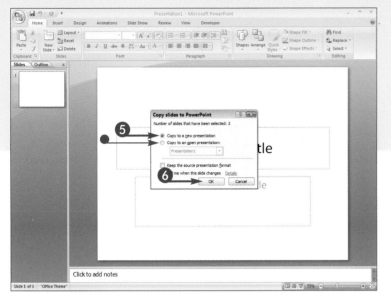

The Copy slides to PowerPoint dialog box appears.

⑤ Click the Copy to a new presentation option (◎ changes to ⦿).

● If you want to copy the slides to an existing presentation, instead, click Copy to an open presentation (◎ changes to ⦿), and then select the presentation you want to use from the Presentation list.

⑥ Click OK.

PowerPoint creates the new presentation and adds the slides.

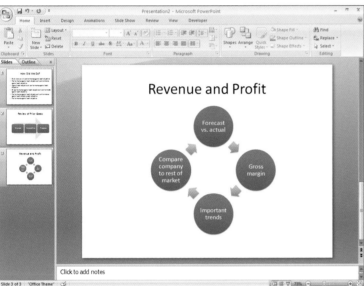

 TIPS

Did You Know?

Each slide in a slide library maintains three properties: the slide's name, presentation, and description. To change any of these properties, position the mouse pointer over the slide name and then click the drop-down arrow. In the list that appears, click Edit Properties. Modify the Name, Presentation, and Description, and then click OK.

Did You Know?

You can make changes to a slide from the slide library. Position the mouse pointer over the slide name, click the drop-down arrow, and then click Edit in Microsoft Office PowerPoint. If you do not want other people to access the slide while you work on it, click the Check Out command, instead.

TRANSLATE WORDS
from within PowerPoint

You can translate words from one language to another by using the Research Task Pane in PowerPoint. The Research Task Pane enables you to see translation results in various forms, such as nouns, verbs, or adjectives. The next time you select the Translation option on the Research Task Pane, the languages chosen on the last search are presented again, so that it is not necessary to repeat language selections unless you want to change the languages to use for the translation.

Translation results appear in the Research Task Pane to the right of the PowerPoint work area. This allows you to continue working while you translate words. You can reposition the Research Task Pane by clicking and dragging it to another area on the screen.

The Research Task Pane also displays additional fee-based options for translation services. You can use the built-in translation tool for translating a few words. For longer documents, however, machine or human translation services can be more accurate.

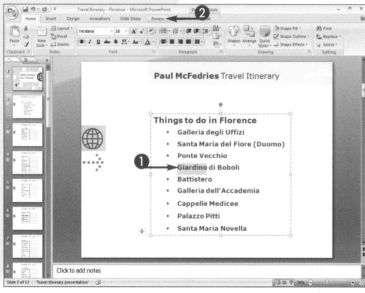

① Select the word you want to translate.

② Click the Review tab.

③ Click Translate.

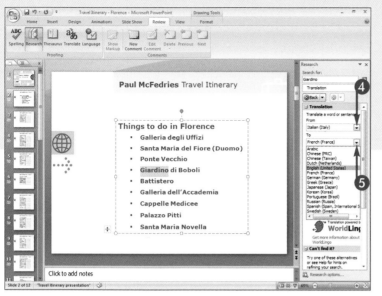

The Research Task Pane appears with the Translation option selected.

④ Click here and select the language from which you want to translate the word.

⑤ Click here and select the language to which you want to translate the word.

DIFFICULTY LEVEL

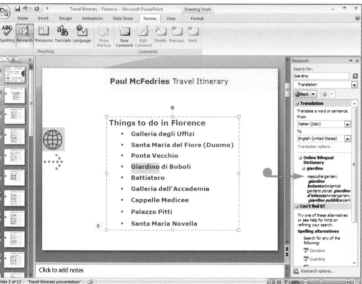

● The translation results appear in the Research Task Pane.

TIPS

Caution!

You may be prompted to install translation services if you have not done so already. If prompted, click Yes to install the services. For example, the first time you use the Research Task Pane to translate a word from Spanish to German, you may be prompted to install the service. Afterward, the Bilingual Dictionary is accessible.

More Options!

If there are languages you never use, you can remove them from the Translation pane and make it easier to select the languages you want. In the Translation pane, click Translation options and then click to deactivate the check box beside each language pair you do not use.

Turn your presentation into a
POWERPOINT TEMPLATE

You can convert a favorite presentation into a PowerPoint Template that you can use to create new presentations. After you create a custom PowerPoint Template, it is made available along with the built-in templates in the New Presentation dialog box.

Custom PowerPoint Templates are especially useful if you have spent time customizing a presentation with the background colors, images, fonts, formatting, and graphics you like. Instead of copying and pasting an existing presentation, and then taking the time to replace all of the content, you can create a new

PowerPoint Template and use as the foundation for a new presentation.

You can also create custom PowerPoint Templates that are variations of an existing template. For example, you may find that you like a particular template, but want to change the color scheme and fonts to match your company's preferences. Instead of using the default template and changing it each time, you can make your modifications once and then save them as a custom PowerPoint Template.

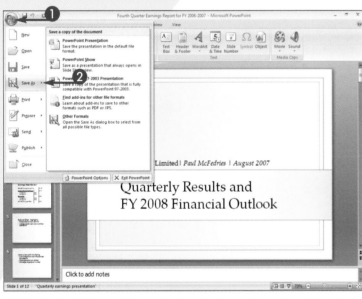

SAVE A PRESENTATION AS A CUSTOM POWERPOINT TEMPLATE

① Click the Office button.

② Click Save As.

The Save As dialog box appears.

③ Use the Save as type list to click PowerPoint Template.

④ Type the name of your custom Design Template in the File name field.

⑤ Click Save.

Your presentation is saved as a custom PowerPoint Template.

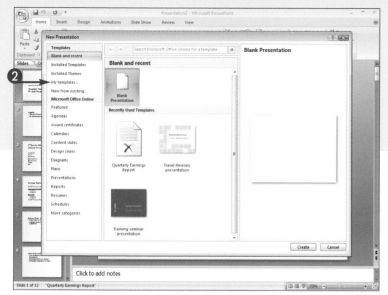

38

① Press Ctrl+N.

The New Presentation
dialog box appears.

② Click My templates.

DIFFICULTY LEVEL

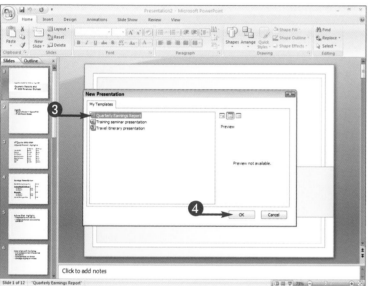

③ Click your custom PowerPoint Template.

④ Click OK.

PowerPoint creates a new presentation
based on the custom template.

Did You Know?

PowerPoint Templates are stored on your
hard drive. For example, your Windows
Vista templates are in the %UserProfile%\
AppData\Roaming\Microsoft\Templates
folder. PowerPoint opens this folder
automatically in the Save As dialog box
when you select the PowerPoint Template
file type. Do not save the template in any
other folder or it will not appear in the
New Presentation dialog box.

Remove It!

If you no longer use a PowerPoint Template,
you should delete it to reduce clutter in the
New Presentation dialog box. Follow Steps **1**
and **2** on this page, right-click the template
you no longer use, and then click Delete.
When PowerPoint asks you to confirm,
click Yes.

Configure Security Settings to
RUN MACROS

If you want to run VBA macros to automate tasks, you must first configure PowerPoint's macro security settings to enable macros.

Visual Basic for Applications (VBA) is a powerful programming language, but its power is all too often used for nefarious ends — such as viruses — so PowerPoint comes with VBA macros disabled as a security precaution. To run macros — even your own macros — you need to adjust PowerPoint's macro security to enable macros.

The easiest way to do this is to enable all macros to run. This is the best option if you never open presentations created by other people, or if you have a good anti-virus program that you use to scan all third-party files before opening them.

Alternatively. You can disable all macros except those that are digitally signed, which ensures authenticity and security. In this case, to run your own macros you need to digitally sign your VBA projects. Office 2007 comes with a tool that enables you to create your own security certificate for the purposes of signing your own VBA projects.

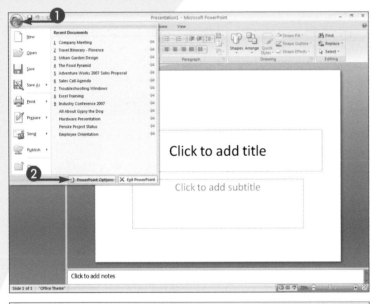

① Click the Office button.

② Click PowerPoint Options.

The PowerPoint Options dialog box appears.

③ Click Trust Center.

④ Click Trust Center Settings.

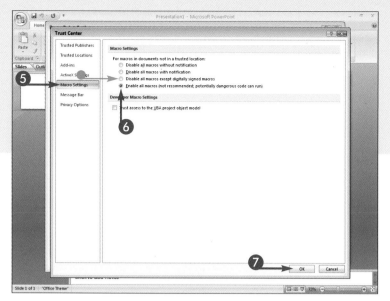

The Trust Center dialog box appears.

⑤ Click Macro Settings.

⑥ Click the Enable all macros option (◎ changes to ◉).

● If you want to run only signed macros, click the Disable all macros except digitally signed macros option (◎ changes to ◉) instead.

⑦ Click OK.

#39

DIFFICULTY LEVEL

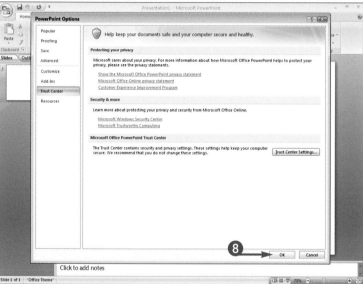

⑧ Click OK.

![TIPS]

Try This!
To create a digital certificate for your VBA projects, click Start, All Programs, Microsoft Office, Microsoft Office Tools, Digital Certificate for VBA Projects. In the Create Digital Certificate dialog box, type your name, click OK, and then click OK when Office tells you the certificate was created.

Try This!
If you create a digital certificate as described in the previous tip, you now need to apply the certificate to each VBA project. Pres Alt+F11 to open the Visual Basic Editor, click the project you want to certify in the Project pane, click Tools, and then click Digital Signature. Click Choose, click your certificate, click OK, and then click OK again.

Chapter 4: Using Timesaving Tools

CREATE A MACRO
in the Visual Basic Editor

If you have a macro that you want to create or copy, you need to add the VBA code for the macro to a module in the Visual Basic Editor.

As you become familiar with manipulating PowerPoint using VBA, you will likely come up with many macro ideas for simplifying complex tasks and automating routine and repetitive chores. To implement these macro ideas, you need to type your code into a new or existing module.

Similarly, you may run across a macro that you want to use for your own work, either as-is or by

modifying the code to suit your needs. In this case, you need to copy the VBA code and then paste it in a new or existing module.

For both operations, you use the Visual Basic Editor, which is the Office 2007 tool for creating and editing VBA code. The Visual Basic Editor is part of PowerPoint, as well as the other major Office applications (Word, Excel, Access, Outlook, and Publisher).

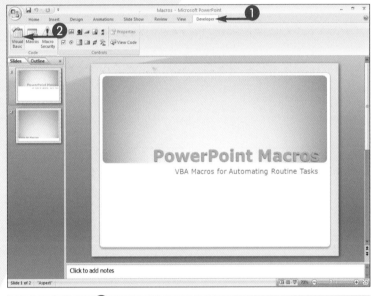

① Click the Developer tab.

Note: If you do not see the Developer tab, see the first tip on the following page.

② Click Visual Basic.

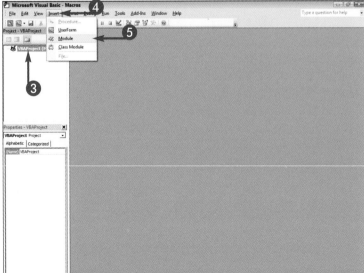

The Visual Basic Editor appears.

③ Click the project to which you want to add the macro.

④ Click the Insert tab.

⑤ Click Module.

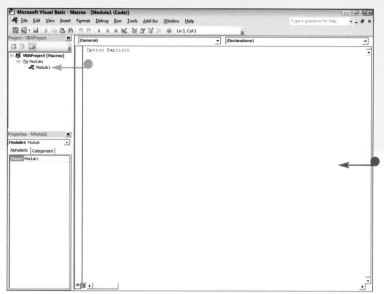

- The Visual Basic Editor adds a new module to the project.

- The Visual Basic Editor opens the new module for editing.

40

DIFFICULTY LEVEL

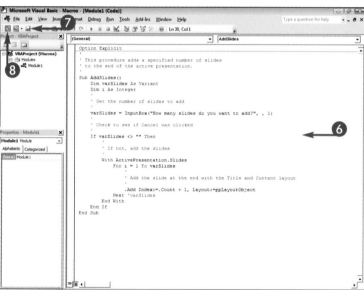

⑥ Type or paste the VBA code in the module.

⑦ Click the Save button.

⑧ Click the View Microsoft PowerPoint button.

The Microsoft Visual Basic Editor closes.

Try This!

The Developer tab is probably the easiest way to run macros and access the Visual Basic Editor. To display it, click Office and then click PowerPoint Options to open the PowerPoint Options dialog box. Click Popular and then click to activate the Show Developer tab in the Ribbon check box. Click OK. Note that this adds the Developer tab to all the Office programs that use the Ribbon.

Did You Know?

After you create a module in a project, you can continue to add new VBA procedures to that module. Follow Steps **1** and **2** to open the Visual Basic Editor, double-click the project you want to work with, and then double-click the module to which you want to add the macro.

RUN A MACRO
to automate your functions

You can easily run a macro that helps automate common functions. Macros are commands that instruct PowerPoint to perform tasks that you would normally accomplish with mouse clicks and keyboard operations.

Macros are most commonly used to automate tasks that would otherwise require multiple steps or require accessing multiple menus or toolbars. For example, you could use a macro to insert a picture, resize the picture, and add a border around it every time the macro is run. Writing macros takes some expertise, but running a macro requires only a few steps.

Macros can greatly help save time and make working with programs like PowerPoint more efficient, but they have also proven to be a great way to spread computer viruses. You should enable and use macros only in presentations you or another trusted person create, or programs that come from a company that has digitally signed it. Digital signatures come from certification authorities and allow you to find the vendor that produced a macro or program if there are virus or other security issues with it.

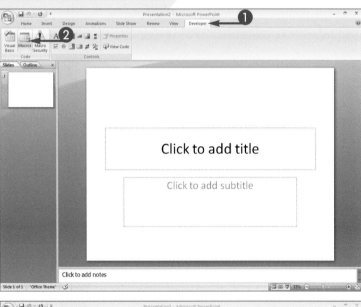

1 Click the Developer tab.

2 Click Macros.

Note: If you do not have the Developer tab displayed, you can also click View and then Macros, or you can press Alt+F8.

The Macro dialog box appears.

3 Click here and select All open presentations.

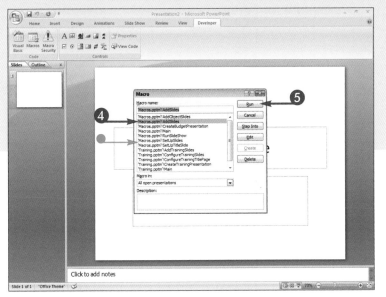

- The available macros appear in the list.
- **4** Click the macro you want to run.
- **5** Click Run.

41

DIFFICULTY LEVEL

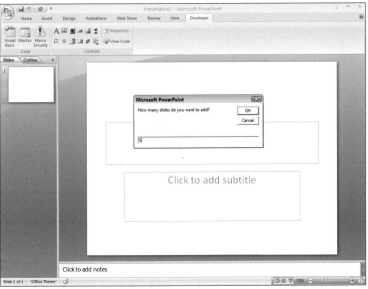

PowerPoint runs the macros. In this example, the macro displays a dialog box to ask how many slides are to be inserted into the current presentation.

TIPS

Did You Know?

You can also run a macro from the Visual Basic Editor. Click Developer and then click Visual Basic (or press Alt+F11). In the Visual Basic Editor, open the project you want to work with and then double-click the module that contains the code. Click anywhere inside the macro, click Run, and then click Run Sub/UserForm (or press F5).

Try This!

You can add a macro to PowerPoint's Quick Access Toolbar. First, switch to the presentation that contains the macro. Click Office, click PowerPoint Options, and then click Customize. Use the Choose commands from list to click Macros. Click the macro you want to add to the toolbar, click Add, and then click OK.

Add Sizzle to Your Presentation with Effects

You can use effects on your slides to create presentations that sizzle. You can apply a shadow effect to transform an image that blends into the background into something that appears to pop off the slide.

You can anticipate questions and prepare to answer them when you insert hyperlinks in text or images that link to other places in your presentation. You can even create a button that opens another program and another document when clicked.

You can create visually stunning presentations that use animation effects to add movement and interest. You can also add entrance or exit effects to text or graphics to help explain complex concepts or illustrate relationships. For example, you can demonstrate sequences of events when you bring a Shape into a slide, explain it, and then click to remove the Shape and simultaneously replace it with another. In fact, you can choreograph multiple effects to occur on each slide just when and where you want them.

You can make your presentations look more professional by using transition effects to gracefully remove one slide and replace it with another. To enhance your presentation even more, you can apply a sound effect to a transition.

Top 100

Highlight graphics when you use
CUSTOM SHADOWS

You can create shadow effects to help make objects and images stand out on your slides. Shadow effects are colored duplicates of an object that are placed behind the object to appear like shadows. Shadow effects give objects depth and often help differentiate them from their background. For example, if your presentation uses a theme and you want to use an image or graphic that is similar in color to the background, the object may appear to fade into the background instead of providing the visual focus you want.

You can add shadow effects to images, Shapes, and even text. You can also use semitransparent shadows that allow the slide's background color to show through the top layer.

Themes in your presentation use default shadow colors, giving the shadow effects a look that coordinates with the other elements in your presentation. After you have added a shadow effect, you can reposition the shadow to appear where you want it.

① Click the image or graphic to which you want to apply a shadow.

② Click the Format tab.

③ Click Picture Effects.

④ Click Shadow.

⑤ Click the shadow effect you want to start with.

● PowerPoint applies the shadow.

⑥ Click Picture Effects.

⑦ Click Shadow.

⑧ Click Shadow Options.

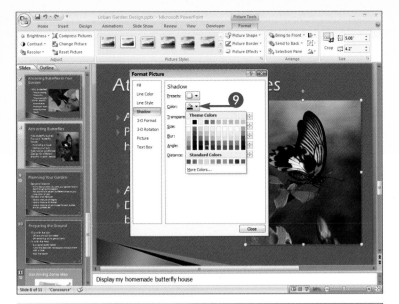

The Format Picture dialog box appears.

⑨ Click here and select the shadow color you want to use.

● Drag ⬚ to set the shadow transparency.

● Drag ⬚ to set the shadow blur.

● Drag ⬚ to set the shadow's distance from the image.

⑩ Click Close.

PowerPoint applies the shadow options.

TIPS

Caution!

You should use care when you add semitransparent shadow effects. Because the background color shows through, sometimes results can be unexpected. For example, if your slide background color is yellow and you add a semitransparent blue shadow effect, the shadow will appear green. The yellow and blue blend together to yield green.

Did You Know?

You can apply a shadow to text. First, click inside the container that holds the text you want to format, and then click Format and Shape Effects. You can now follow Steps **7** to **10** from this task to apply the shadow and its options.

Did You Know?

You can use the Format Painter to apply your new shadow effect to other objects. For more information about using the Format Painter, see Task #33.

CREATE A LINK
to go elsewhere in the presentation

You can quickly navigate to a specific slide in your presentation with a click of your mouse. PowerPoint automatically creates a bookmark, or a targeted place to link to in your presentation, based on the presentation's outline. Bookmarks are created for each slide in your presentation. You can easily identify which slide to link to because each slide is listed by a slide number and a slide title. When you create a hyperlink that links to another place in your presentation, you are also creating a hyperlink to a bookmark in the presentation.

Hyperlinks to different parts of your presentation work when you deliver your presentation in Slide Show view. By default, hyperlinks appear on-screen as underlined text, and when you click them, the linked slide automatically appears. Hyperlinks to other locations in your presentations can be particularly convenient when you anticipate questions at specific points in the presentation. You can click the hyperlink to quickly shift to the other slide to help answer those questions.

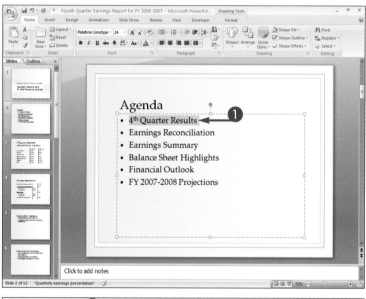

1 Click and drag to highlight the text to which you want to add a hyperlink.

2 Click the Insert tab.

3 Click Hyperlink.

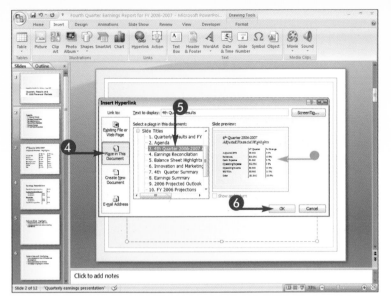

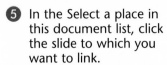

The Insert Hyperlink dialog box appears.

④ Click Place in This Document.

⑤ In the Select a place in this document list, click the slide to which you want to link.

● A preview of the slide appears here.

⑥ Click OK.

DIFFICULTY LEVEL

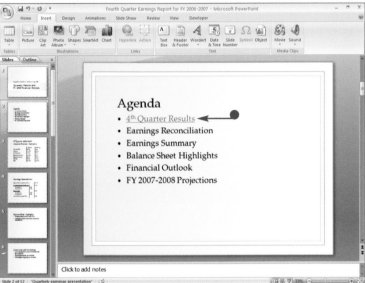

● PowerPoint adds the hyperlink to the slide.

TIPS

Did You Know?
You can link graphics and shapes to other parts of your presentation. Click the object you want to link and then follow Steps **2** to **6** in this task.

Apply It!
You can also create a hyperlink to the previous or next slide. Follow the steps in this task, but in Step **5**, click Next Slide or Previous Slide instead of clicking a specific slide.

Apply It!
You can assign a ScreenTip to each hyperlink. A ScreenTip is a text banner that appears when you position the mouse over a hyperlink. Follow Steps **1** to **5** above and then click ScreenTip. Type the ScreenTip text you want to use and then click OK.

OPEN A DOCUMENT
with the click of a button

You can open a document in a separate program without leaving PowerPoint when you create an action button. Action buttons are graphical buttons that you can draw onto a slide. You can assign actions to the buttons to perform key tasks. Creating an action button that opens a document allows you to stay in Slide Show view while the other program opens. This is much more convenient than exiting the Slide Show, minimizing PowerPoint, starting the other program, and then opening the document.

Action buttons are convenient because you can create them from within PowerPoint; it is not necessary to use a separate graphics creation tool to create great-looking buttons. You can create them to be as large or small as you want.

When you give your presentation, click the button and the program opens with the file you specified. Action buttons that open files can be very useful when you want to be able to refer to a document quickly if needed, such as a brochure, a contract, or a database.

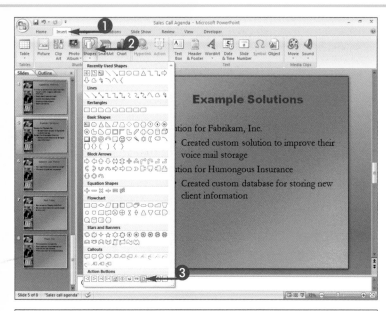

① Click the Insert tab.

② Click Shapes.

③ Click the action button you want to use.

④ Click and drag to indicate a size for the action button.

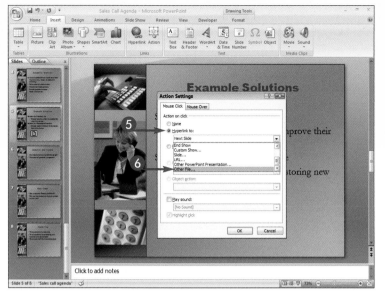

When you release your mouse, PowerPoint draws the action button and displays the Action Settings dialog box.

⑤ Click Hyperlink to (◯ changes to ◉).

⑥ Scroll down and click Other File.

The Hyperlink to Other File dialog box appears.

⑦ Navigate to the folder that contains the document you want to link to.

⑧ Click the document.

⑨ Click OK.

⑩ Click OK.

PowerPoint creates the action button with a link to open the document you specified.

TIPS

More Options!

To use an action button to run a different program, follow Steps **1** to **4**, then click the Run program option. Click Browse, use the Select a Program to Run dialog box to click the file that runs the program, and then click OK. Most programs install in the Program Files folder on the Windows hard drive (usually drive C).

More Options!

To use an action button to open a different PowerPoint presentation, follow the steps in this task and select a presentation file in Step **8**. Alternatively, follow Steps **1** to **5** and then click Other PowerPoint Presentation. In this case, PowerPoint displays the Hyperlink to Other PowerPoint Presentation dialog box, which just shows PowerPoint files. Follow Steps **7** to **10**.

ADD MOTION
to illustrate your content

You can add motion paths to graphics to draw attention to your content and help illustrate key points in your PowerPoint presentations. Motion paths allow you to bring normal text or graphics onto your slide in linear, curved, or free-form shapes. When you deliver your presentation, the images enter the screen in the path or shape you have chosen.

Adding motion to graphics is a great way to focus attention on an important logo or graphic because the eye is naturally drawn to movement. It is also a good way to create effects like those produced with

Macromedia Flash without using a separate tool or learning a separate program.

You can also apply more than one motion path to an image, each starting after you click your mouse. For example, you could have one part of a diagram slide into place, discuss it, and then click your mouse for the next part of the diagram to slide in, using the motion path you specified.

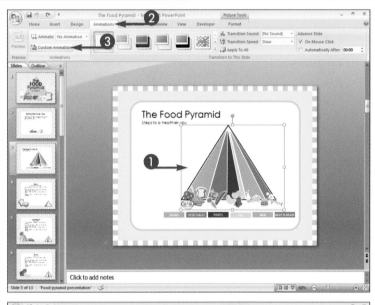

1. Click the object you want to animate.

2. Click the Animations tab.

3. Click Custom Animation.

The Custom Animation task pane appears.

4. Click Add Effect.

5. Click Motion Paths.

6. Click Draw Custom Path.

7. Click Curve.

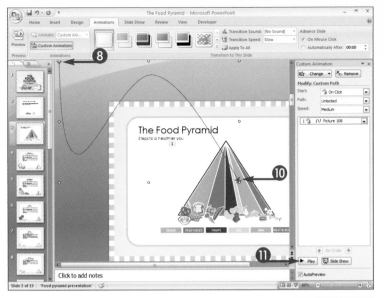

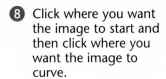
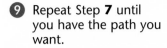

8 Click where you want the image to start and then click where you want the image to curve.

9 Repeat Step **7** until you have the path you want.

10 Double-click at the end of the motion path.

The motion path appears on the screen and the action is listed in the Custom Path section of the Custom Animation Task Pane.

11 Click Play.

PowerPoint previews the animation for you.

TIPS

Try This!

If you have multiple motion paths in a single slide, you can choose to start the motion paths one after another instead of waiting for a click before each effect begins. In the Custom Animation task pane, click the motion path you want to work with, and then use the Start menu to click After Previous.

Change It!

If you are not satisfied with the shape of the curve you drew, you can change the shape to something more suitable. In the Custom Animation task pane, click the motion path you want to work with. PowerPoint adds selection handles around the frame of the motion path. Click and drag these handles to change the shape of the curve.

Make an entrance with
CUSTOM ANIMATIONS

You can help illustrate important points better when you create *builds* out of graphics and text. A build is an animation sequence that displays a slide's content by bringing in one element at a time. Builds allow you to add an element into a slide, discuss it, and then click when you are ready for the next element to enter. This is particularly useful when presenting diagrams that have multiple parts, each requiring explanation.

Conveniently, it is not necessary to create a separate slide for each part of the build; all of the build

elements make up a single slide. When printed, the slide looks like the final result of the build.

You can choose from among many entrance styles for each effect. Each entrance style gives the effect a completely different look. You can continue to add entrance effects to each element on the slide until each element appears when desired.

The Custom Animation task pane also makes it easy to preview the effects as you build them. When you click the Play button, the Custom Animation plays without entering Slide Show mode.

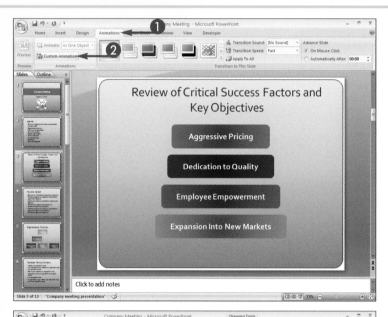

① Click the Animations tab.

② Click Custom Animation.

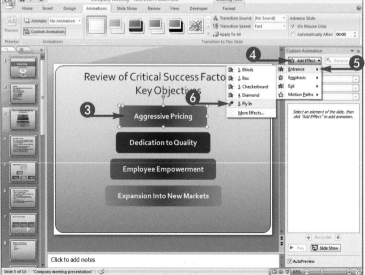

The Custom Animation task pane appears.

③ Click the object you want to animate.

④ Click Add Effect.

⑤ Click Entrance.

⑥ Click Fly In.

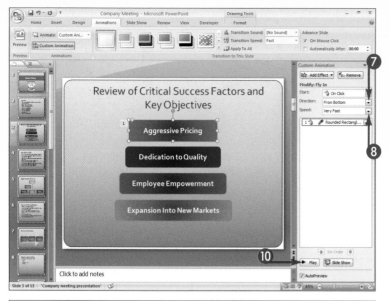

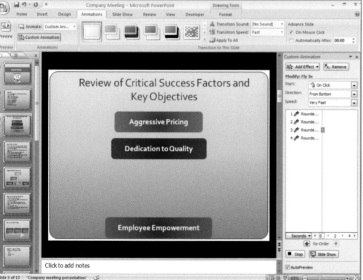

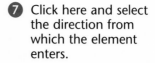

DIFFICULTY LEVEL

PowerPoint adds the effect to the Custom Animation task pane.

⑦ Click here and select the direction from which the element enters.

⑧ Click here and select the speed at which you want the effect to occur.

⑨ Repeat Steps **3** to **8** for each effect you want to add.

⑩ Click Play.

The animation plays for you.

TIPS

Important!
It is usually easier to first create your slide with all text and graphics placed where desired, and then go back and create the build effects. This ensures that all of the slide elements fit together when the builds have completed.

Try This!
If you want to create a build with an object that has multiple parts, such as a SmartArt graphic or a chart, first apply the animation to the entire object. In the Custom Animation task pane, right-click the effect and then click Effect Options. In the *Object* Animation tab (such as SmartArt Animation), use the Group Graphic list to click One by one, and then click OK.

Orchestrate an exit with
CUSTOM ANIMATIONS

You can create impressive presentations when you use builds to have text or graphics exit from your slide by clicking your mouse. Using exit effects can help viewers focus on topics that are currently being discussed as the previous topics are removed.

You can also use exit effects to generate excitement on slides. For example, you can use a combination of entrance and exit effects to display and then remove customer quotes or positive feedback to help give your slide visual impact and a feeling of excitement about the products or services being discussed.

If you use exit effects frequently, you can change effect styles for variety. For example, one image could exit using the Checkerboard style, and one text area could exit using the Diamond style.

By default, exit effects occur at high speed. However, you can set exit effects to take place more slowly for a more subtle style. You can create multiple exit effects on each slide, and after each build, you can preview your exit effects from within the Custom Animation task pane.

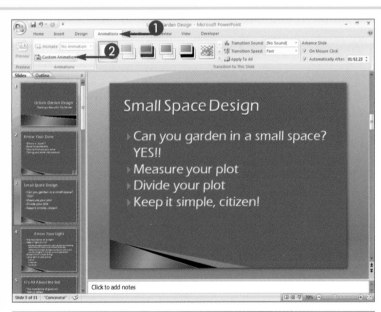

① Click the Animations tab.

② Click Custom Animation.

The Custom Animation task pane appears.

③ Select the text or click the object you want to animate.

④ Click Add Effect.

⑤ Click Exit.

⑥ Click the effect you want to apply.

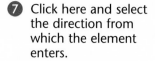
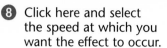

47

PowerPoint adds the effect to the Custom Animation task pane.

⑦ Click here and select the direction from which the element enters.

⑧ Click here and select the speed at which you want the effect to occur.

⑨ Repeat Steps **3** to **8** for each effect you want to add.

⑩ Click Play.

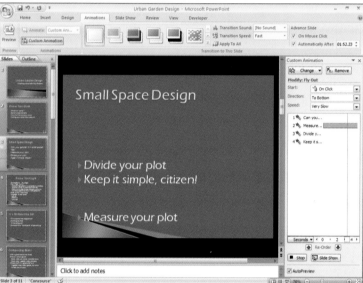

The animation plays for you.

TIPS

Change It!

You can change the order in which exit effects take place. After following the steps above, click the effect you want to reorder, and then click the Re-Order arrows until the effect is in the position you prefer.

More Options!

Exit effects can occur one after another instead of after you click your mouse. Follow Steps **1** to **6**, use the Start list to click After Previous, and then follow steps **7** to **10**.

Did You Know?

If you are applying effects to a number of slide elements, the preview that PowerPoint runs after you apply each effect can slow you down. Click to deactivate the AutoPreview check box to prevent PowerPoint from previewing each effect.

Choreograph effects to make a
MULTIMEDIA PRESENTATION

You can create visually interesting presentations that help you tell a story when you choreograph effects. Choreographed effects can have different start or stop times and can include entrance effects, exit effects, motion paths, or even audio or video.

For example, if you want to illustrate a timeline of events, you could bring in a graphic, discuss it, and then bring in another graphic as the one you just discussed exits the screen. When you want to discuss complex topics, choreographing effects can help you break them down into pieces that are easier to understand.

After each effect is created, it is listed in the Custom Animation task pane, where you can determine whether the effect begins with a mouse click or whether it begins after the previous effect is completed. This is very useful when you want to illustrate how pieces fit together by displaying one piece, then another immediately thereafter. You can choose the speed at which effects occur.

① Click the Animations tab.

② Click Custom Animation.

The Custom Animation task pane appears.

③ Select the text or click the object to which you want to apply an entrance effect.

④ Click Add Effect.

⑤ Click Entrance.

⑥ Click the effect you want to apply.

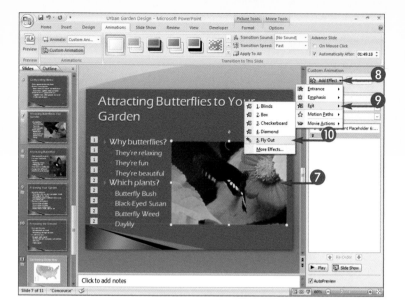

The effect is added to the object.

⑦ Click the object to which you want to add an exit effect.

⑧ Click Add Effect.

⑨ Click Exit.

⑩ Click the effect you want to apply.

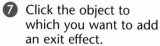

48

DIFFICULTY LEVEL

The exit effect is added to the object.

⑪ Click here and select After Previous from the Start menu.

⑫ Click here and select a speed from the Speed menu.

⑬ Repeat Steps **3** to **12** for each object on which you want to apply an effect.

⑭ Click Play.

PowerPoint plays your arranged effects.

TIPS

Did You Know?
If you have more than one element that you would like to enter or exit at the same time, you can group the elements first and then apply the effect. Ctrl+click to select multiple items such as text or graphics, and then follow the steps above.

Try This!
You can orchestrate effects so that they occur at the same time. Follow the steps above, but in Step **11**, click With Previous instead of After Previous.

More Options!
You can change the order in which exit effects take place. After following the steps above, click the effect to reorder and then click the Re-Order arrows to move the effect to its desired position.

Give your presentation a professional look with
TRANSITION EFFECTS

You can give your presentations a more polished look when you apply transition effects between your slides. Transition effects determine what happens between the time you click your mouse to advance to the next slide and the time the next slide loads.

By default, presentations do not use transition effects. When you click your mouse to advance a slide during the slide show, the next slide simply appears on the screen. However, PowerPoint gives you many professional-looking transition effects you can apply

to your slides. For example, the Dissolve effect removes blocks of your slide and then rebuilds it with the next slide.

When you apply a transition effect, you can see how it will look from within the Animations tab. This saves time because it is not necessary to view your presentation in Slide Show mode in order to see how the effect will look.

After you apply the transition effect to your slides, you can adjust the speed at which it occurs.

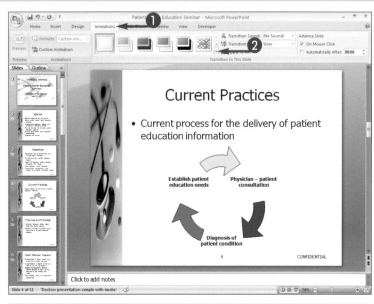

① Click the Animations tab.

② Click here.

The Transition gallery appears.

③ Click a transition effect.

A preview of the transition appears on the slide.

④ Click here and select the speed at which you want the transition to appear.

⑤ Click Preview.

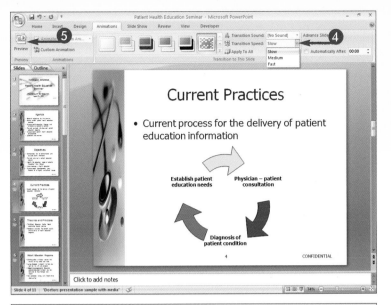

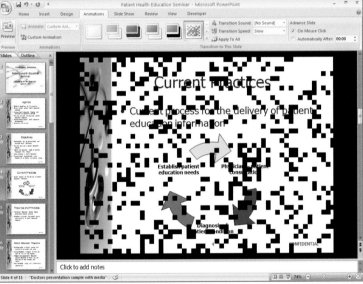

The slide plays in Slide Show mode with the desired transition.

Try This!

It is usually best not to use too many different transitions in a presentation. In fact, most effective presentations use only a single transition throughout. However, applying the transition to every slide individually is time-consuming. Instead, set up the transition for a single slide as described in this task and then click Apply to All.

Automate It!

You can automate your presentation to advance each slide after a predetermined number of seconds. Click the Animations tab and then click the Automatically After check box. Use the associated spin box to set the number of seconds after which you want the slide to advance to the next one.

Enhance a transition with a
SOUND EFFECT

You can apply a sound to one or more slides in a presentation. PowerPoint 2007 comes with nearly 20 built-in sound effects that you can use with your transitions. For example, you can apply the Drum Roll sound effect before an announcement slide or the Applause sound effect before a congratulatory slide. If you have a custom animation that brings the slide title on one letter at a time, you can run the Typewriter sound effect during the transition. Other built-in sounds include Bomb, Camera, Cash Register, Explosion, and Wind.

If you have your own sound effect that you would prefer to use, PowerPoint enables you to choose a sound file, as long as that file uses the WAV sound format.

When used appropriately, transition sounds highlight important information during a slide show. As a rule of thumb, using transition sounds sparingly means the sounds will have greater impact, increasing audience attention to the most important information. Having the same sound for every slide has less impact.

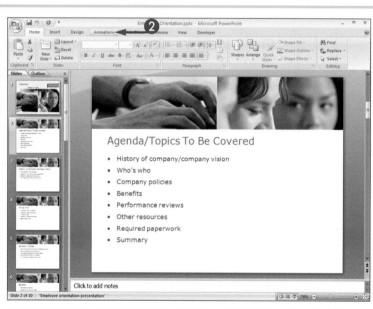

1 Display the slide to which you want to add the transition sound.

2 Click the Animations tab.

3 Click the Transition Sound menu.

● To use one of PowerPoint's built-in sounds, click a sound effect in the list.

4 Click Other Sound.

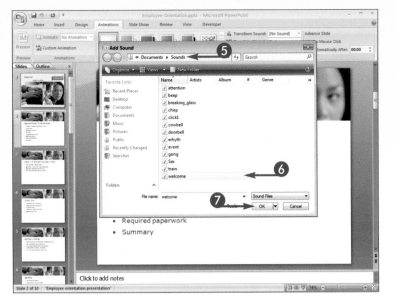

5 Navigate to the folder that contains the sound file.

6 Click the sound file.

7 Click OK.

DIFFICULTY LEVEL

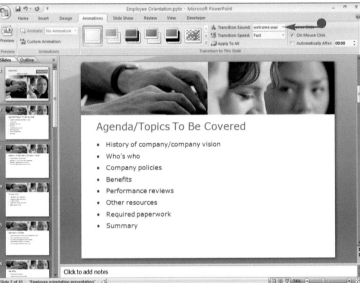

PowerPoint previews the sound.

● The name of the sound file appears in the Transition Sound box.

TIPS

More Options!

By default, PowerPoint plays the transition sound file only once. That is usually fine for longer sound effects, but it may not allow a shorter sound to have much of an impact. To have PowerPoint repeat the sound, click the Transition Sound menu and then click the Loop Until Next Sound command to activate. To stop the sound during the slide show, right-click the slide.

More Options!

If you activated the Loop Until Next Sound option as described in the previous tip, the sound will keep playing until the next sound effect is played. If your next slide does not have a sound effect, you can still get PowerPoint to stop the previous sound. Display the next slide, click the Transition Sound menu, and then click [Stop Previous Sound].

6

Communicate with Audio and Video

You can enhance your presentations with audio and video to improve communication. Audio and video can come from a variety of sources, such as recordings from previous presentations, audio and video from the Clip Art Gallery, and even CDs.

You can play audio and video clips in a separate player, or you can embed the player into your slide so that the audio or video clip looks like it is part of the slide. Because Microsoft Windows Media Player comes with Windows, it is the player used in this chapter.

The key to getting audio and video to play or record properly in PowerPoint is to first get the audio to play or record properly outside

PowerPoint. After your audio/video capabilities are set up on your computer, you can use PowerPoint to record the audio for your presentation and automatically match that audio with each slide. This enables your viewers to listen to your audio at the same time they view your presentation.

If you want an audio or video clip to play only when you are ready for it, you can create a button that plays a clip when clicked. You can also play a sound when you position your mouse pointer over an object, or you can loop audio so it repeats indefinitely. You can also choreograph multiple sound or video effects on a slide to produce a professional presentation that gets your work noticed.

Top 100

ADD A BUTTON
to play your video clip

You can add a button to your slide that, when clicked, plays a video clip in Windows Media Player. This is a great way to play video clips only when you are ready for them. For example, if you are delivering a presentation about an event and you are not sure if you will have time to play your video clip, you can insert a button onto the slide that plays the video only when it is clicked.

The button you create is an action button. In this case, the action is to play a specific video file using Windows Media Player. To launch the video clip, you must know the path to the file. In Windows Vista, for example, the default folder for video and movies is named Videos, which is located in your user profile folder. Its path is usually C:\Users*Name*\Videos, where *Name* is your user name.

In PowerPoint 2007, the ability to run programs via an action button is disabled as a security measure. Therefore, when you run the action button, you will need to tell PowerPoint that it is okay to run the program.

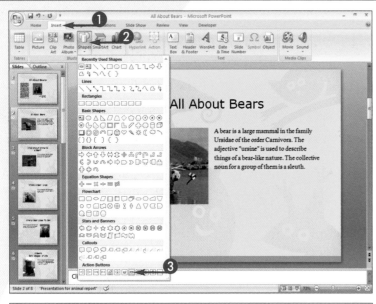

① Click the Insert tab.

② Click Shapes.

③ Click the Movie action button.

④ Click and drag where you want to position the button.

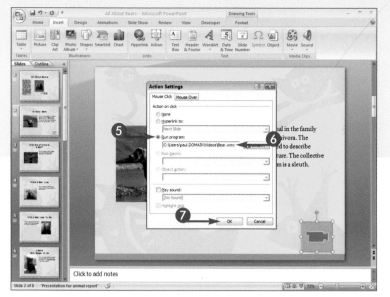

PowerPoint creates the button and displays the Action Settings dialog box.

⑤ Click Run program (◉ changes to ◉).

⑥ Type the path to your video file.

⑦ Click OK.

PowerPoint assigns the play video action to the button.

⑧ Press F5 to open the presentation in Slide Show view.

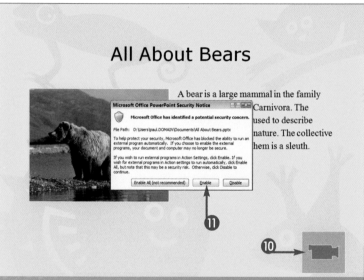

The presentation opens in Slide Show view.

⑨ Navigate to the slide that contains the action button.

⑩ Click the action button.

⑪ If you see a security warning, click Enable.

Note: PowerPoint blocks links to external programs because those programs might install viruses. You know that your video is not malicious, however, so you can safely click Enable.

The video plays.

TIPS

Did You Know?

You can also browse to the file you want to open instead of typing the path. After Step **5**, click Browse. In the Select a Program to Run dialog box, click Programs and then click All Files. Now navigate to the folder in which the video file resides, click the file, and then click OK. Then proceed with Step **7**.

Try This!

You can use a different player program by preceding the video file path with the path of the file that starts the program, followed by a space. You can find the path to the program by clicking Start, All Programs, and then right-clicking the program for which you want to find the path. Click Properties and then click the Shortcut tab. The location appears in the Target field.

EMBED VIDEO
to turn your slide into a movie

You can use video clips in your presentations to help tell a story. Video delivers more impact when it is integrated into your slide. For example, if your presentation is designed to train viewers on a particular topic, you can incorporate a video file into your slide to allow them to see the video, which you can start, pause, and restart just by clicking your mouse.

You can make the video even more useful when you add a bulleted list of text next to it to highlight key

points. When you embed the video into your slide, you are given more control over positioning and the ability to see other content as well as the video at the same time.

When you insert the video file into your slide, the Ribbon adds a Movie Tools section with an Options tab that enables you to adjust various settings for the video. For example, you can decide whether the video starts playing when you click it or automatically when you display the slide.

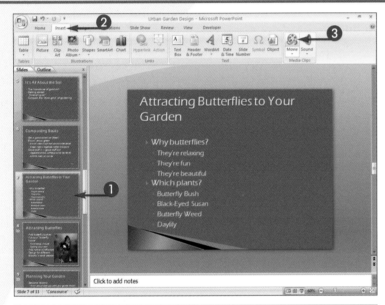

1 Display the slide into which you want to insert the video.

2 Click the Insert tab.

3 Click the top half of the Movie button.

The Insert Movie dialog box appears.

4 Navigate to the folder that contains your video file.

5 Click the video file.

6 Click OK.

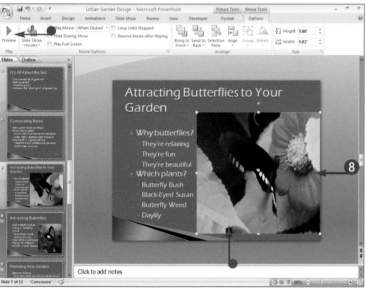

PowerPoint asks you how you want the video to start.

⑦ Click When Clicked.

● If you prefer that the video start as soon as you display the slide, click Automatically, instead.

● PowerPoint inserts the video file.

⑧ Click and drag the sizing handles to resize the video object to fit into your slide.

● You can click Preview to see how the video looks on your slide when it plays.

More Options!

If the original video is large, it may not look good if the video object is too small on your slide. Click Options and then click to activate the Play Full Screen check box to have the video take up the entire screen while it plays.

More Options!

If your video comes with sound, you can control the volume that plays during the slide show. Click Options, click Slide Show Volume, and then click the relative volume you prefer (Low, Medium, High, or Mute).

More Options!

If your video is short, you may prefer to have it repeat until you click it. To set this up, click Options and then click to activate the Loop Until Stopped check box.

ADD SOUND
from a file

You can make your presentations more interesting by adding audio clips that contain entertaining or informative content. For example, if you are holding a conference and want to display a welcome slide in the front of the room while attendees get settled, you can add an audio clip that plays music while the slide is on the screen. Additionally, if you are presenting a slide that discusses how happy customers are with your product, you can insert directly into the slide an audio clip of a customer talking about your product to really emphasize your points.

When you insert an audio clip from a file, a small audio icon is placed onto the slide. That audio icon can be clicked and dragged to the desired location on the screen. When you are ready for the audio clip to play while you are in Slide Show mode, you simply click the audio icon and the audio plays. You can also have PowerPoint play the sound automatically when you display the slide. The audio clip does not play in an external media player; it plays through your computer's audio system.

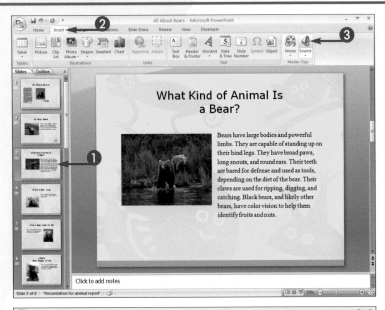

① Display the slide into which you want to insert the sound.

② Click the Insert tab.

③ Click the top half of the Sound split button.

The Insert Sound dialog box appears.

④ Navigate to the folder that contains your sound file.

⑤ Click the sound file.

⑥ Click OK.

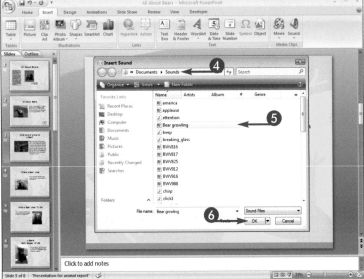

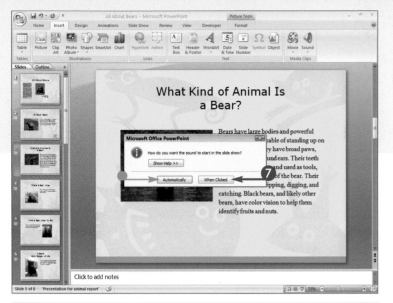

PowerPoint asks you how you want the sound to start.

⑦ Click When Clicked.

● If you prefer that the sound start as soon as you display the slide, click Automatically, instead.

#53

DIFFICULTY LEVEL

PowerPoint inserts the sound icon.

⑧ Click and drag the sound icon to position it where you want in your slide.

● You can click Preview to hear the sound.

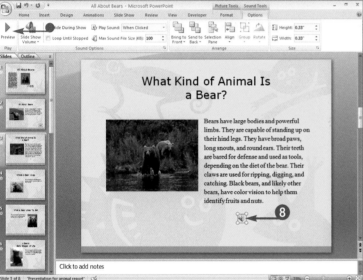

TIPS

More Options!

If your sound file is lengthy, you can configure the sound to play across multiple slides until it finishes. Click Options, click the Play Sound menu, and then click Play across slides.

More Options!

You can control the volume that the sound file uses during the slide show. Click Options, click Slide Show Volume, and then click the relative volume you prefer (Low, Medium, High, or Mute).

More Options!

If you configured the sound to play automatically when you display the slide, you might not want the sound icon to appear during the slide show. To set this up, click Options and then click to activate the Hide During Show check box.

LOOP
an audio file

You can use looped audio to play music or a message repeatedly in your presentations. Looped audio is repeated from beginning to end until it is interrupted. Looped audio can be particularly useful in presentations where you display a slide indefinitely. For example, if you plan to display a slide during a break in a conference, you may want to play music or an instructional message for the duration of the break. Adding a looped audio file to the slide will allow you to walk away from the presentation assured that the audio will continue to play until you are ready to begin again.

You can also use looped audio to lengthen a short sound effect, such as a drum roll. You can have the audio loop for as long as you need it to play, then interrupt it by clicking the slide.

You can set up an audio file to loop after you have inserted it, as described in Task #53. In the current task, you will learn how to insert and loop a sound clip from the Clip Organizer.

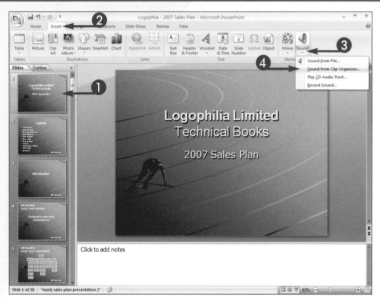

1. Display the slide into which you want to insert the sound clip.

2. Click the Insert tab.

3. Click the bottom half of the Sound split button.

4. Click Sound from Clip Organizer.

   Note: If you see a dialog box asking whether you want to include clips from Microsoft Office Online, click Yes.

The Clip Art pane appears.

5. Click the sound clip you want to insert.

PowerPoint asks you how you want the sound to start.

⑥ Click When Clicked.

● If you prefer that the sound start as soon as you display the slide, click Automatically, instead.

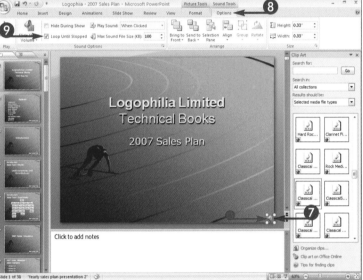

54

● PowerPoint inserts the sound icon.

⑦ Click and drag the sound icon to position it where you want in your slide.

⑧ Click Options.

⑨ Click Loop Until Stopped (☐ changes to ☑).

The looped audio is set to play in your presentation.

TIPS

Preview It!

If you are not sure which sound clip to use, PowerPoint enables you to preview any clip before inserting it. In the Clip Art pane, right-click a clip and then click Preview/Properties. PowerPoint displays the Preview/Properties dialog box and plays the sound clip. Click Play to hear the clip again. Click Close when you are done.

Caution!

If you think your sound clip will loop many times, make sure you pick a clip that will not become tiresome or annoying after awhile. Also, make sure the sounds at the beginning and the end of the clip are relatively harmonious. This ensures that the transition from one loop to another is not too jarring.

Boost your presentation with
AUDIO FROM A CD

You can enhance your presentation with audio and save time when you play audio directly from a CD. It is not necessary to upload music to your computer's hard drive in order to play it from PowerPoint. Instead, you can instruct PowerPoint to play audio directly from the CD player in your computer.

For example, if you want to play music from a CD before and after a seminar and during breaks, you can insert audio into introductory, break, and conclusion slides to play directly from a CD. You can even specify exactly what tracks on the CD you want to play.

You can also choose to loop audio to play repeatedly until it is interrupted. For example, you could choose to continually play tracks 1 through 4 of a CD until interrupted during a break. The audio can be interrupted when you click to advance to the next slide.

When you deliver your presentation, a CD symbol is inserted into the slide that can be clicked to start playing the audio again from the beginning.

1 Display the slide into which you want to insert the CD audio.

2 Insert the audio CD.

Note: If Windows asks what you want to do with the audio CD, click Close.

3 Click the Insert tab.

4 Click the bottom half of the Sound split button.

5 Click Play CD Audio Track.

The Insert CD Audio dialog box appears.

6 Use the Start at track spin box to click the track number at which you want to start.

7 Use the End at track spin box to click the track number at which you want to end.

8 Click Loop until stopped (changes to ✓).

9 Click OK.

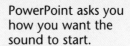

PowerPoint asks you how you want the sound to start.

⑩ Click Automatically.

● If you prefer that the sound start only when you click the icon, click When Clicked, instead.

● PowerPoint inserts the CD audio icon.

⑪ Click and drag the icon to position it where you want in your slide.

● You can click Preview to hear the audio CD tracks you selected.

TIPS

Caution!

When you deliver your presentation, PowerPoint plays audio from whatever CD is in your computer's CD player. If you design your presentation with one CD in mind, but the CD player has another CD in it when you deliver your presentation, you could get unexpected results.

Caution!

You should make sure that the license agreement that came with your CD allows you to play the music in public forums.

Did You Know?

You can play only a selected part of an audio track. After you have inserted the audio CD icon, click the Options tab. In the Start Playing box, use the Time spin box to set the time at which the first track begins. In the Stop Playing box, use the Time spin box to set the time at which the last track ends.

INSERT AN AUDIO BUTTON
in your slide

You can add depth to your presentations when you insert audio clips into your slides. You can make the effects look even more professional when you create buttons that link to audio clips.

Placing a button on a slide with an audio symbol makes it more obvious to presenters or viewers that supplemental audio is available for a slide. For example, when you place an audio clip onto a slide, a very small audio symbol is normally inserted. It is small enough that it could be missed by the presenter

and the viewer. When you create an audio button, it draws attention to the fact that there is an audio clip available for the slide.

Audio buttons are added to the slide by creating an action button, which is a professional-looking image that you can draw onto your slide in whatever size you want. They are called action buttons because you can assign actions that make them interactive, such as linking to an audio file when the button is clicked.

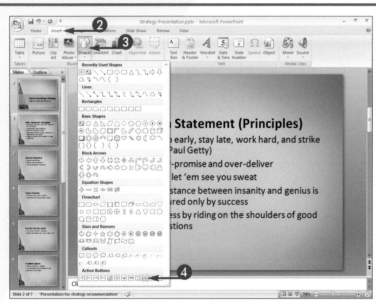

① Display the slide into which you want to insert the action button.

② Click the Insert tab.

③ Click Shapes.

④ Click the sound action button.

⑤ Click and drag where you want to position the button.

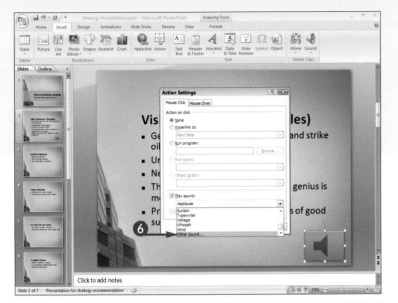

PowerPoint creates the button and displays the Action Settings dialog box.

⑥ Click here and select Other Sound.

The Add Sound dialog box appears.

⑦ Navigate to the folder that contains the sound file.

⑧ Click the sound file.

⑨ Click OK.

PowerPoint previews the sound file.

⑩ Click OK.

PowerPoint assigns the sound file to the action button.

Change It!

You do not always have to use the same sound with the action button. If you want to use a different sound, click the action button, click Insert, and then click Action to open the Action Settings dialog box. Follow Steps **6** to **10** in this task to select a new sound file.

Did You Know?

The color of the action button is determined by the design theme you are using on the slide. If you change the theme, PowerPoint changes the action button color to match. To change the button format by hand, click it, click the Format tab, and then use the controls in the Shape Styles group.

Hover your mouse to
PLAY A SOUND

You can enhance the entertainment value of text or images when you apply an effect that plays a sound when you hover your mouse over the object. For example, if you have a slide that announces the winners of a skateboarding contest, you can add impact and a festive feeling if viewers hear applause when you hover your mouse over a picture of the winning skateboarders. In the same way, on a slide presenting great photos, you can apply the sound of a camera clicking when you hover your mouse over each image.

You can add hover sounds to text or images by using action settings. Action Settings enable you to create hyperlinks, run programs, run macros, or apply sound effects like Applause, Arrow, Bomb, Breeze, Camera, Cash Register, and Chime. You can also apply more than one effect to an object, such as the launch of a video clip and a sound effect at the same time you hover over an object.

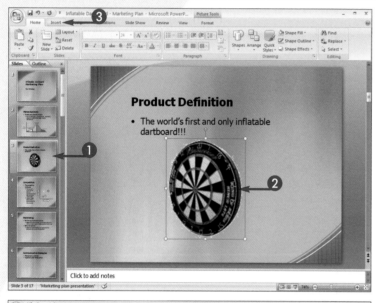

① Display the slide into which you want to insert the action button.

② Click the image to which you want to add the mouseover sound.

③ Click the Insert tab.

④ Click Action.

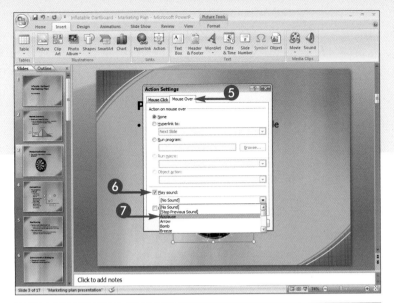

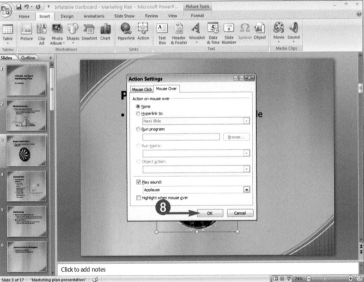

PowerPoint displays the Action Settings dialog box.

⑤ Click the Mouse Over tab.

⑥ Click Play sound (☐ changes to ☑).

⑦ Click the sound effect you want to play.

DIFFICULTY LEVEL

⑧ Click OK.

PowerPoint assigns the sound file to the image's mouseover action.

Did You Know?

You can also choose to apply audio effects to run when clicked instead of hovered over. Follow the steps above, but omit Step **5**.

Try This!

The hover effect works when you are viewing your presentation in Slide Show mode. Click Slide Show, click From Current Slide to open the slide in Slide Show mode, and then position the mouse pointer over the image to hear the sound.

More Options!

You can configure PowerPoint to make the image appear as though it has been "clicked" when you hover the mouse over it. Follow Steps **1** to **7**, click to activate the Highlight when mouse over check box, and then click OK.

RECORD NARRATIONS
for your slides

You can prepare your presentation for use when you are not there by recording narrations for your slides. The Record Narration tool enables you to record audio for your presentation, and afterward, when the presentation is viewed in Slide Show mode, your audio accompanies the slide.

You can save time by using the Record Narration tool because it not only helps you record the audio for your presentation, it keeps track of the timing for each slide and then automatically advances to the next slide at the appropriate time. For example, if

you want others to be able to view your presentation on their own, you can use Record Narration to record your voice for each slide, synchronized to advance to the next slide at just the right time.

When you choose to link narrations to a location on your hard drive, the audio file for each slide is stored separately on your computer. This keeps the file size down and keeps performance high. If you choose not to link narrations, the audio is stored with the presentation.

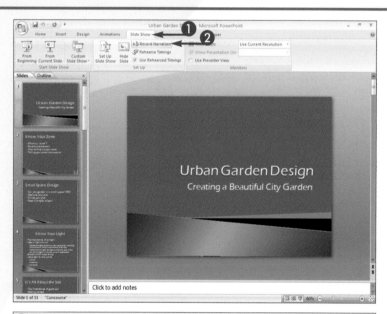

1 Click the Slide Show tab.

2 Click Record Narration.

The Record Narration dialog box appears.

● To have PowerPoint save the narration as separate audio files, click Link narrations in (☐ changes to ☑).

3 Click OK.

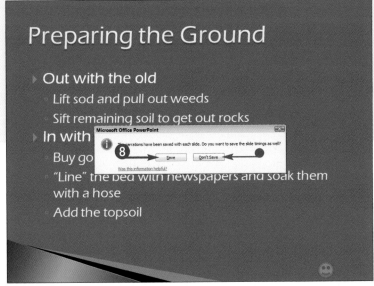

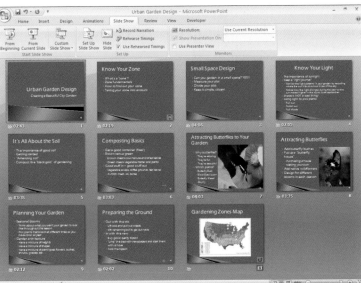

The presentation opens in Slide Show mode.

④ Give your presentation while recording audio into your microphone.

⑤ Press the spacebar to advance to the next slide.

⑥ Repeat Steps **4** and **5** for all the slides to which you want to record narrations.

⑦ Press the Esc key when you have finished recording.

The Microsoft Office PowerPoint dialog box appears.

⑧ Click Save.

● If you made a mistake during the recording, click Don't Save, instead, and then start over.

PowerPoint switches to Slide Sorter view and displays the timings for each narration under each slide.

TIPS

Change It!

Because each person's voice and volume varies, you will need to adjust most microphones to the correct levels before recording. PowerPoint includes tools to optimize recording. To access these tools, before Step **3** above, click the Set Microphone Level button in the Record Narration dialog box.

Caution!

You can set quality levels to determine the richness of the audio recording. Although everyone wants the best quality possible, high-quality recordings take more hard disk space and make file sizes larger. To adjust levels to give you the best quality for the bandwidth or file size available, before Step **3** above, click the Change Quality button in the Record Narration dialog box.

Create a
NARRATED SLIDE SHOW

You can go back and match audio clips with slides in a presentation that has been recorded. After you match the audio clip with each slide, the audio clip plays automatically when the slide opens.

For example, if one of your company's executives delivers a presentation at a conference where the audio is recorded, you can package that presentation so that viewers can listen to the audio clip from the presentation at the same time they view the slides. This is a great way to deliver training materials, to

circulate the presentation's message broadly, and to leverage existing resources.

First, split the recording of the presentation into separate audio files, where there is one audio file for each slide's audio. After the audio files are created, each slide is edited to insert the audio clip for that slide. In addition, you can hide the audio symbol when delivering the presentation in Slide Show mode to keep your slides clean and uncluttered.

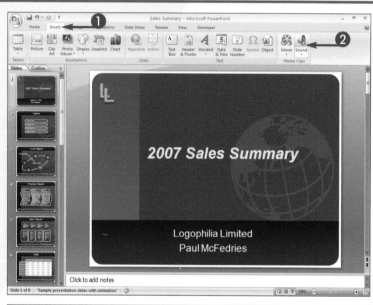

① Click the Insert tab.

② Click the top half of the Sound split button.

The Insert Sound dialog box appears.

③ Navigate to the folder in which the audio clip file is located.

④ Click the audio file you want to match to this slide.

⑤ Click OK.

The Microsoft Office PowerPoint dialog box appears.

⑥ Click Automatically.

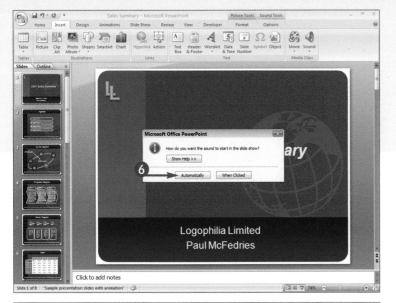

PowerPoint inserts the audio icon into the slide.

⑦ Click the Options tab.

⑧ Click Hide During Show (☐ changes to ☑).

⑨ Repeat Steps **1** to **8** for each slide to which you want to add an audio clip.

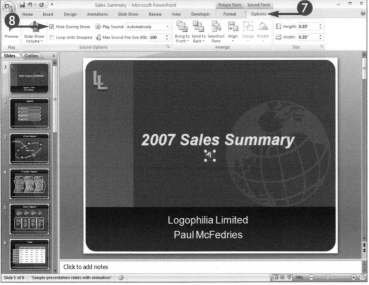

TIPS

Try This!

You can choose to play the audio when clicked instead of automatically. In Step **6** above, click When Clicked instead of Automatically, and then proceed with Step **7**. Omit Step **8**, or you will not be able to see the audio icon on which to click.

Did You Know?

When you insert audio files into your presentation, they are stored in the presentation itself. When there are many audio files or the audio files are very large, your presentation file size increases. If it becomes too big, you may want to consider using Record Narration instead because you can link to audio files instead of embedding them in the presentation. See Task #58 for more information about Record Narration.

Produce a professional presentation when you
SYNCHRONIZE EFFECTS

You can use PowerPoint to produce a professional multimedia presentation. Multimedia presentations include audio, video, and effects. PowerPoint can help you synchronize all of them to play when and where you want.

For example, a slide can contain a transition effect, an audio file to play when the slide is loaded, and an entrance effect to make a graphic enter slowly at a small size and then expand to its normal size. You can coordinate each of these effects to play at just the right time and for the desired duration.

You can use the Custom Animation task pane to reorder effects and change the speed at which they occur. You can also use the timeline to click and drag fields that represent the beginning and end times for an effect, enabling you to move them where you want in a graphical and easy-to-use fashion. Additionally, you can set effects to occur simultaneously with the previous effect, after the previous effect is finished, or upon clicking the mouse.

① Click the Animations tab.

② Click Custom Animation.

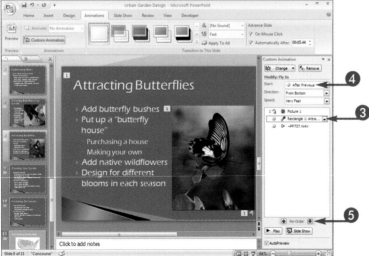

The Custom Animation task pane appears.

③ Click here and select the effect with which you want to work.

④ Click here and select After Previous.

⑤ Click the Re-Order arrows until the effect is in the desired order.

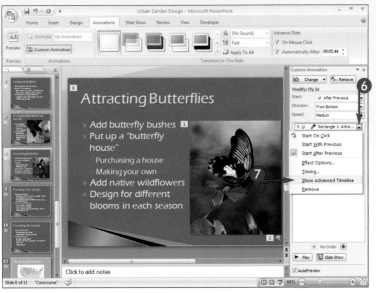

6 Click the drop-down arrow beside the effect with which you want to work.

7 Click Show Advanced Timeline.

● PowerPoint displays the Advanced Timeline.

● This box shows you where the effect begins (represented by the left edge) and ends (the right edge).

8 Click and drag the left edge to adjust the start time of the effect.

9 Click and drag the right edge to adjust the end time of the effect.

10 Repeat Steps **3** to **5** and Steps **8** and **9** to set the timing of the other effects.

Caution!
Because audio files have a fixed duration, you cannot click and drag the end point of an audio file displayed in the Custom Animation task pane to extend its play. Instead, you can loop the audio to make it repeat. For more information about looping audio, see Task #54.

Apply It!
When you click the Play button on the Custom Animation task pane, you can see a preview of all of the effects on the slide.

Did You Know?
If your animations take a long time, you can scroll the advanced timeline by clicking the left and right arrows. For a lengthy series of animations, you might find it easier to work with a larger timeline interval. To configure the timeline in this way, click Seconds and then click Zoom Out.

Enhance Your Presentations with Custom Content

You can communicate more effectively when you use specialized content to illustrate important information or concepts. You can include hyperlinks to Web pages in your presentations to bring in information and resources on demand to answer questions that arise. You can even include hyperlinks to e-mail addresses so that potential customers can easily reach you.

The Equation Editor can make fast work out of typing and formatting equations. You can also insert symbols to represent characters that are not on your keyboard, such as ®, ©, or ™.

If you work with financial or statistical data, you can put it to good use by inserting it into your slide from a Microsoft Excel spreadsheet.

You can even insert Excel functionality into your presentation if you want to display data that requires calculations. You can also graphically communicate numerical data in your slides by inserting an Excel-based chart.

You can use diagrams more effectively when you connect shapes to form lines or arrows between objects. These lines stay connected even when you move the objects. You can also use the Organization Chart to update your organizational changes.

If you use a Tablet PC to create or edit your presentations, you can use Ink Annotations to make free-form notes or sketches directly onto your slides.

Top 100

LINK TO THE WEB
from your presentations

You can create hyperlinks to pages or sites on the World Wide Web to supplement the content in your presentations. These links are available to click when you deliver your presentation in Slide Show view. The hyperlinks are underlined so that you can differentiate them from normal text. When you click the link, your Internet browser opens with the Web page loaded.

You can also create hyperlinks to pages on your company's intranet site. For example, in a presentation about company sales performance, you

can include links to supplemental sales data in case detailed questions are asked about the points in your slides. Likewise, when giving a presentation about your company's marketing efforts, you can include a link to your company's Web site and internal marketing sites.

You can also add hyperlinks to graphics, shapes, or other objects on your slides. To create a hyperlink on a graphic or shape, follow the steps below, but in Step **1**, click the graphic or shape, and then proceed with Step **2**.

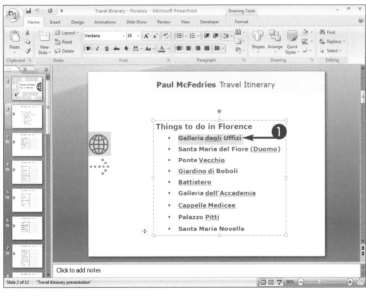

1 Select the text to which you want to add the hyperlink.

2 Click the Insert tab.

3 Click Hyperlink.

136

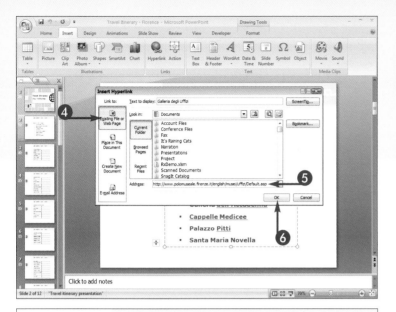

The Insert Hyperlink dialog box appears.

④ Click Existing File or Web Page.

⑤ Use the Address text box to type the address of the Web page you want to link to.

⑥ Click OK.

Paul McFedries Travel Itinerary

Things to do in Florence

- **Galleria degli Uffizi** ←
- **Santa Maria d** (http://www.polomuseale.firenze.it/english/musei/uffizi/Default.asp)
- **Ponte Vecchio**
- **Giardino di Boboli**
- **Battistero**
- **Galleria dell'Accademia**
- **Cappelle Medicee**
- **Palazzo Pitti**
- **Santa Maria Novella**

The Insert Hyperlink dialog box closes.

⑦ Press F5 to view the slide in Slide Show mode.

● The slide appears in Slide Show mode with the hyperlink.

TIPS

Change It!

By default, when you position your mouse pointer over the hyperlink, the target URL appears. If you want it to display different text, follow Steps **1** to **5** above, and then click the ScreenTip button. Type the desired text in the ScreenTip text box in the Set Hyperlink ScreenTip dialog box, and then click OK.

Try This!

The easiest way to insert the hyperlink into the Address field in the Insert Hyperlink dialog box is to start in the browser with the Web page loaded. Select and copy the address line displayed in your browser. In Step **5** above, click inside the Address text box and then press Ctrl+V to paste the address.

Add a link to an
E-MAIL ADDRESS

You can make it easy for customers or potential customers to reach you when you include hyperlinks to your e-mail address in presentations. Links to e-mail addresses look just like regular hyperlinks, with underlined text to differentiate it from regular text. When the presentation is in Slide Show mode, the hyperlink is clickable.

When links to e-mail addresses are clicked, the viewer's default e-mail client is opened, a new e-mail message is created, and the message is preaddressed to the e-mail address specified. When

viewers finish with the e-mail message, they must intentionally return to PowerPoint to complete viewing the presentation, so you might want to include links to e-mail addresses at the end of your presentation so you do not risk losing viewers before they are finished with the presentation.

You can also specify the subject line for use by those sending a message. For example, to easily identify messages received from clicking the link, you can specify a subject line, such as Patient Health Education Seminar.

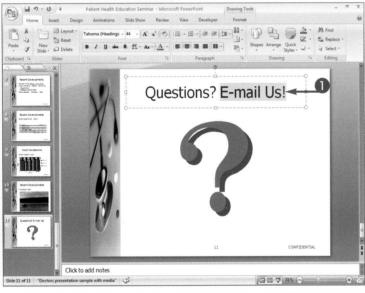

① Select the text to which you want to insert the e-mail hyperlink.

② Click the Insert tab.

③ Click Hyperlink.

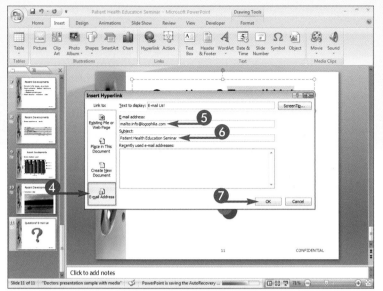

The Insert Hyperlink dialog box appears.

④ Click E-mail Address.

⑤ In the E-mail address field, type the complete e-mail address of the message's intended recipient.

⑥ In the Subject field, type the subject of the message.

⑦ Click OK.

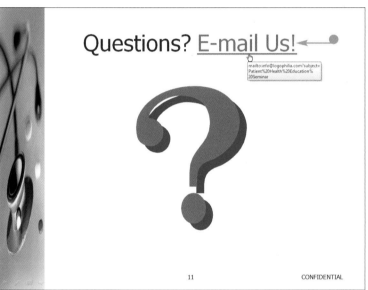

The Insert Hyperlink dialog box closes.

⑧ Press F5 to preview the slide in Slide Show mode.

● The presentation opens in Slide Show mode with the hyperlink inserted onto the slide.

Did You Know?

A hyperlink is also differentiated from normal text by its font color. If your presentation does not use a design theme, hyperlinks are blue by default. If your presentation does use a design theme, the Design tab's Colors button determines the hyperlink font color.

Change It!

When you position your mouse pointer over a hyperlink to an e-mail address while in Slide Show mode, it appears as "mailto:<alias> subject:<subject>," which is hardly a user-friendly ScreenTip. To change the ScreenTip to something friendlier, follow Steps **1** to **5**, and then click the ScreenTip button. Type the new ScreenTip text in the ScreenTip text box in the Set Hyperlink ScreenTip dialog box, and then click OK.

Explain it better with
EQUATIONS

If presenting material that contains equations is part of your job, you know that creating and formatting equations can be cumbersome because they can include symbols, characters, and shapes that are not found on a standard keyboard and would take significant time to draw by hand. The Equation Editor, which is a program that comes with PowerPoint, eases the creation and editing of equations.

Although Word 2007 includes an enhanced tool for creating equations, that tool is not available in PowerPoint. However, PowerPoint does support the Equation Editor, which enables you to insert Equation Editor objects into your slides.

The Equation Editor enables you to type formulas or parts of formulas from samples that look like the equation you seek to create and to easily insert equation-specific symbols and characters. These range from mathematical operators to logical symbols to uppercase and lowercase Greek letters. You can choose from templates for fences, fractions, radicals, subscripts, superscripts, summations, integrals, underbars, overbars, and more.

① Navigate to the slide in which you want to insert the equation.

② Click the Insert tab.

③ Click Object.

The Insert Object dialog box appears.

④ Click Microsoft Equation 3.0.

⑤ Click OK.

The Equation Editor window appears.

6 Type your equation.

7 Click File.

8 Click Exit and Return to *Document*, where *Document* is the name of your PowerPoint presentation.

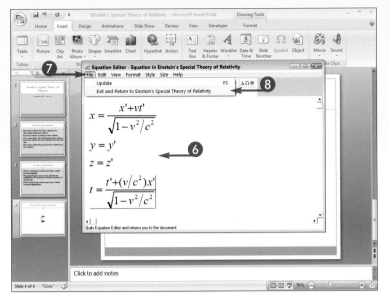

PowerPoint adds the equation to the slide.

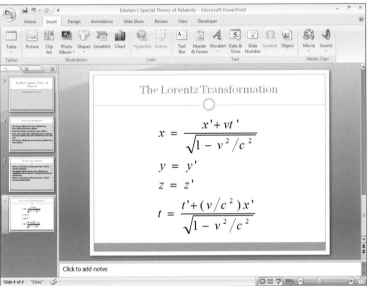

Customize It!

PowerPoint usually inserts an Equation Editor object in a frame that is too small to read the equation properly. Click and drag the corners and sides of the object to enlarge it enough to make the equation readable.

Did You Know?

After you insert an Equation Editor object, you may discover an error or you may want to make changes to the equation. To edit an equation, double-click the Equation Editor object. The Equation Editor window opens with the equation ready for updating.

Caution!

You cannot change the Equation Editor's black font, so you won't be able to see the equation if your slide uses a black background. Create a rectangle with a light color and place the equation on top of it.

Type specialized
CHARACTERS AND SYMBOLS

You can type characters that are not available on your keyboard when you insert symbols into your slides. You can use symbols for business purposes to type special characters like copyright (©), registered trademark (®), or trademark (™). You can also use characters from foreign alphabets or type emoticons, such as ☺ or ☹, to add feeling or emotion to slides.

You can also use symbols to create borders. For example, you can create a border by typing a specific

symbol repeated across the top of a slide. You can also highlight important text with symbols. For example, you can insert an arrow symbol before key items in a bulleted list.

Each font has its own collection of symbols. If you use a specific font in your presentation, you may need to use a different font for the symbol you want to use. For example, if you use an Arial font in your presentation, but you want to insert a check box symbol (☑), you will find it in the Wingdings font.

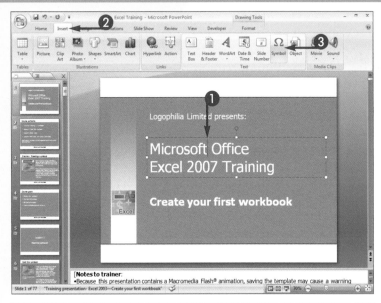

① Click where you want to insert a symbol.

② Click the Insert tab.

③ Click Symbol.

The Symbol dialog box appears.

④ Use the Font list to click the font you want to use.

⑤ Click the symbol you want to insert into your slide.

⑥ Click Insert.

7 Click Close.

8 Repeat Steps **1** to **7** for each symbol you want to insert into your slide.

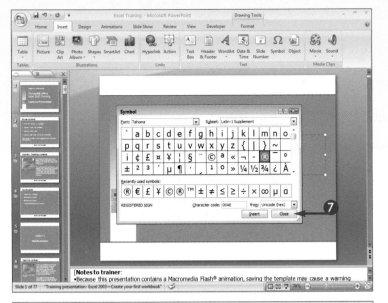

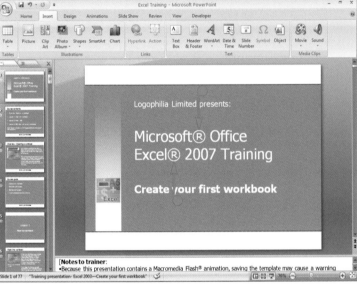

● The symbols appear in your slide.

TIPS

Caution!

If you insert multiple symbols while the Symbol dialog box remains open, they will appear next to one another. If you do not want to have to reopen the Symbol dialog box each time you need a symbol, you can insert all that you will need at one time and in one location, and then cut and paste them to the location desired.

Did You Know?

After you have inserted a symbol, you can change its color, size, and even add shadows, just as you would with any other text. For example, to display the registered trademark symbol as a superscript, select the symbol, click Home, click the Font dialog box launcher, click to activate the Superscript check box, and then click OK.

Add an Excel spreadsheet to
LEVERAGE DATA

You can save time and reduce the need to retype data when you insert an Excel spreadsheet into your slide. Reusing existing Excel spreadsheets reduces the risk of error that is introduced when you retype data. For example, instead of typing sales data into a presentation, you can insert data from an existing Excel spreadsheet directly into your slide.

When you insert an Excel spreadsheet into your presentation, the entire spreadsheet appears in its original format. When you click the object that

represents that file, the menu options change to give you Excel functionality directly within PowerPoint. For example, you can select and delete columns, edit data, and use tools like AutoFormat.

Because most Excel spreadsheets are not designed for presentation on a large screen, you will most likely want to adjust font sizes to make the data easier to read. You can do this by selecting the text and using the standard tools in PowerPoint to increase the font size.

① Navigate to the slide in which you want to insert the spreadsheet.

② Click the Insert tab.

③ Click Object.

The Insert Object dialog box appears.

④ Click the Create from file option.

⑤ Click Browse.

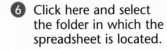

The Browse dialog box appears.

6 Click here and select the folder in which the spreadsheet is located.

7 Click the Excel spreadsheet you want to insert into the slide.

8 Click OK.

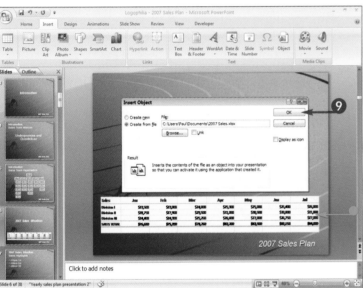

The Insert Object dialog box appears.

9 Click OK.

● PowerPoint inserts the spreadsheet into the slide.

Did You Know?

You can resize the spreadsheet object by clicking and dragging the object borders. If you want to make changes to the data, double-click the spreadsheet object.

Did You Know?

Making changes to the content in the spreadsheet from within PowerPoint does not change the original spreadsheet. Therefore, you can delete columns that are not needed in a specific presentation without changing the original spreadsheet.

Try This!

You can set up a link to the original file so that if the spreadsheet changes, data on the slide automatically changes. To set up the link, follow Steps **1** to **8** above, and then in the Insert Object dialog box, click to activate the Link check box.

Add an Excel spreadsheet to
CALCULATE DATA

You can save time by inserting Excel spreadsheet tools directly into a slide. You can take advantage of the calculation, formatting, conditional formatting, and analysis capabilities in Excel while you continue to do your work in PowerPoint.

If your slides routinely include information that requires calculations, you may be accustomed to using a calculator and then typing the results into a PowerPoint table. Instead, you can insert Excel spreadsheet capabilities directly into the slide so that the calculations take place where the data resides.

For example, in a marketing plan presentation for a new product, you can include a break-even analysis based on the list price of the product and its expected costs. If the price or cost structure changes, you can edit the spreadsheet in the slide and the break-even analysis automatically adjusts for you.

When you are not editing the spreadsheet, it appears as a table on the slide, and the window returns to the standard PowerPoint Ribbon. When you double-click the spreadsheet object to edit it, the Ribbon and other interface options change to their Excel versions.

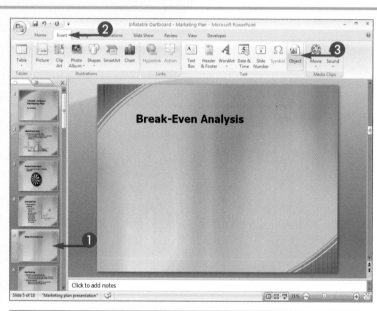

① Navigate to the slide in which you want to insert the spreadsheet.

② Click the Insert tab.

③ Click Object.

The Insert Object dialog box appears.

④ Click the Create new option.

⑤ In the Object type list, click Microsoft Office Excel Worksheet.

⑥ Click OK.

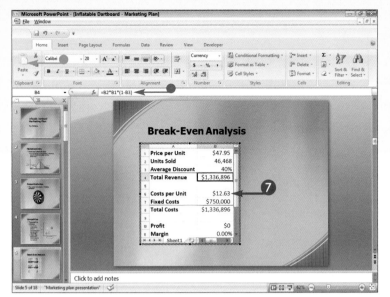

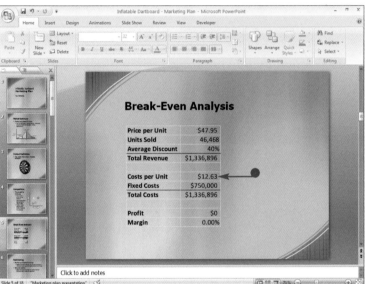

PowerPoint inserts an empty spreadsheet into the slide.

● Excel's Ribbon appears.

● Excel's formula bar appears.

⑦ Type your data and use the formatting and analysis tools as you would in Excel.

⑧ When you are done, click outside the spreadsheet.

DIFFICULTY LEVEL

● PowerPoint displays the Excel spreadsheet as a table.

TIPS

Try This!

After your data is entered into the spreadsheet object, you can apply a theme to give it a professional look. Double-click the spreadsheet object to display the Excel Ribbon, click Page Layout, click Themes, and then click the theme you want to use.

More Options!

Spreadsheet data looks best when the spreadsheet object is no larger than the data it contains. To resize the spreadsheet object, double-click it to display small black squares on the corners and sides of the object. Click and drag any square until the edge is against the existing data. You may need to repeat this for each side you want to resize.

Tell your story with
ILLUSTRATED CHARTS

You can use charts to illustrate important financial or numerical data. Charts help turn data into information, which makes it easier to identify trends and relationships. For example, you can greatly improve a table containing a list of financial results when you turn it into a chart that helps viewers identify variances or areas that need improvement.

PowerPoint charts use Microsoft Excel chart tools, but you do not need to know how to use Excel to be successful in using charts. When you insert a chart

into a slide, a sample chart is inserted with sample data opened in a spreadsheet for you to edit. You can type your data over the sample data, and as you do, the chart updates automatically. This allows you to create a chart to suit your needs without having to create a separate Excel workbook.

The slide's design theme determines the fonts that are used in the charts and the colors that are used on the bars to make your charts blend in with other elements in your slides.

1. Navigate to the slide in which you want to insert the spreadsheet.

2. Click the Insert tab.

3. Click Chart.

The Insert Chart dialog box appears.

4. Click the chart category you want to use.

5. Click the chart type you want to use.

6. Click OK.

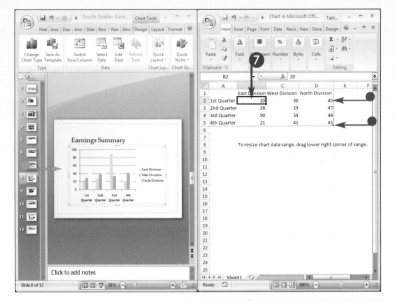

- PowerPoint inserts a default chart into the slide.

- The chart's underlying data appears in an Excel worksheet.

- Click and drag the lower right corner of the range to adjust the size of the charge data range.

DIFFICULTY LEVEL

⑦ Use the worksheet to type the data on which you want to base the chart.

PowerPoint updates the chart automatically with your new data.

⑧ In Excel, click Office.

⑨ Click Exit Excel.

Note: If you prefer to leave Excel running for other tasks, click Close on the Office menu, instead.

The PowerPoint window returns to its normal size and your chart appears in the slide.

TIPS

Change It!
You can change the chart to any of the other chart styles, including Bar, Line, Pie, and more. Click the chart, click the Design tab under Chart Tools, and then click Change Chart Type. In the Change Chart Type dialog box, click a chart category, click a chart type, and then click OK.

Try This!
You can edit the chart data after you have inserted it. Click the chart, click the Design tab under Chart Tools, and then click Edit Data. PowerPoint launches an Excel worksheet and displays the chart data.

Did You Know?
You can change the colors that PowerPoint uses to display the chart data markers. Click the chart, click Design, and then click Colors. Right-click the color scheme you want to use, and then click Apply to Selected Slides.

Make a point when you
CONNECT GRAPHICS

You can connect graphics to help illustrate timelines and relationships. Connectors are straight or curved lines or arrows that connect two or more drawing objects, such as shapes, images, or other graphics. Connectors automatically anchor themselves to the midpoint of a side of an object, saving you time because you no longer have to painstakingly click and drag lines so that they meet exactly at an object's edge.

For example, in a diagram that contains six boxes that illustrate key concepts, you can demonstrate

relationships by drawing an arrow from one box to the next. Similarly, in a flowchart diagram, you can use connector lines to illustrate the movement between tasks, tests, and other components of the flowchart.

Adding connector lines takes only a few mouse clicks, and the connector is automatically anchored to the midpoints on each object with perfectly straight lines connecting them. Even better, if you move one of the objects, the lines stay connected, making editing diagrams easier than ever.

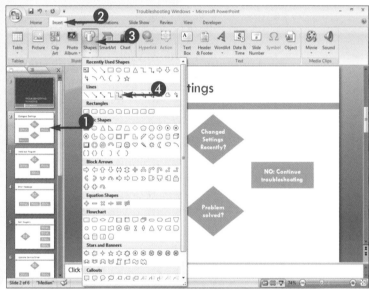

① Display the slide containing the two objects you want to connect.

Note: You can connect shapes, text boxes, WordArt, clip art, pictures, and more.

② Click the Insert tab.

③ Click Shapes.

The Shapes gallery appears.

④ In the Lines section, click the connector style you want to apply.

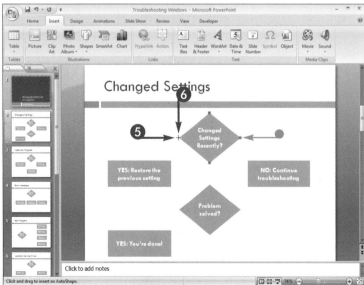

⑤ Position the mouse pointer over the first item.

● Red connector handles surround the object.

⑥ Click the handle you want to use as the anchor point.

PowerPoint establishes the handle you click as the first anchor point.

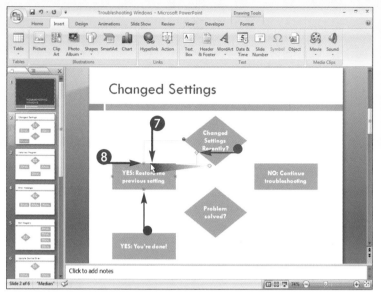

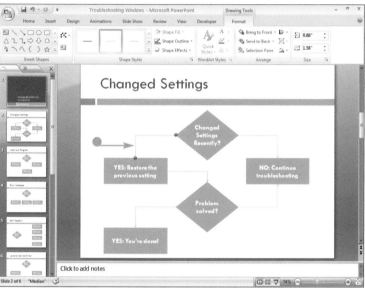

● PowerPoint adds the basic connector shape to the slide.

⑦ Drag the round end of the connector over the object to which you want to connect.

A dashed line trails your connector line as you drag to the other object on the slide.

● Red connector handles surround the object.

⑧ Click the handle you want to use as the second anchor point.

● PowerPoint draws a connector line between the two objects.

You can apply formatting to the connector line using the drawing tools.

⑨ Repeat Steps **2** to **8** to add other connector lines to the slide.

Did You Know?

There are three types of connectors. Straight connectors use a straight line, Elbow connectors use straight lines and right angles, and Curved connectors use curved lines.

Change It!

You can easily move a connector from one object to another. Click the end of the connector you want to move and drag it to another drawing object.

Change It!

If you rearrange drawing objects, and the connectors now connect objects in a path that could be shortened, you can use Reroute connectors to fix the problem. Right-click a connector you want to reroute and click Reroute connectors. The connector changes to take the shortest route between the connected objects.

Show relationships with
ORGANIZATION CHARTS

You can show relationships between employees when you insert an organization chart into your slide. An organization chart is a hierarchical SmartArt graphic that uses shapes to represent team members, and connectors to illustrate the relationships between them.

Using a SmartArt organization chart saves time because it not only creates a sample organization chart for you, it makes it easy to add or remove subordinates, co-workers, or assistants at the appropriate levels in the organization. It also resizes the chart automatically as the number of represented employees grows. Changing the names on organization charts is easy because all you have to do is click the shape and start typing, or use the separate SmartArt text window.

You can also rearrange team members on the organization chart by clicking and dragging their shapes to the desired location. Colors for shapes and the text used on them are determined by the design theme used on your slide. When you are not editing the organization chart, it appears on your slide as the SmartArt Object so you can freely add and edit text and graphics around it.

1 Click the Insert tab.

2 Click SmartArt.

● If you have a content placeholder on the slide, you can also click the SmartArt icon in the placeholder.

The Choose a SmartArt Graphic dialog box appears.

3 Click Hierarchy.

4 Click Organization Chart.

5 Click OK.

PowerPoint inserts a basic organization chart into your slide.

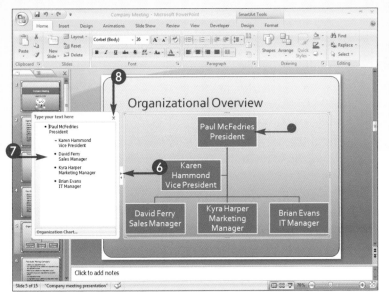

⑥ Click the Show Text button.

⑦ Use the Type your text here window to type the names and positions of the employees.

Note: When typing, press Shift+Enter to start a new line.

⑧ Click Close when you are done.

● Another way to add text is to click inside a shape and then type the text.

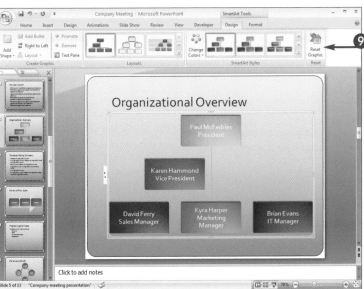

⑨ Use the controls on the Design tab to give the organization chart the layout and look you want.

TIPS

Change It!

You can change the style of the organization chart. Click the shape below which you want to change the layout. If you want to change the layout of the entire organization chart, click the shape representing the highest-level manager. Click Design, click Layout, and then click the style you want to use.

Modify It!

To add more shapes, click an existing shape, click the Design tab, click Add Shape, and then click where you want the shape added. For example, if the employee is below the current employee in the organization, you would click Add Shape Below. Similarly, if the new employee is an assistant, you would click Add Assistant.

Get your presentation noticed with
INK ANNOTATIONS

You can use your Tablet PC with its pen input device to create Ink Annotations. Ink Annotations are like handwritten notes that lie on top of your slides. Ink Annotations can be used in Slide Show mode or while you are editing slides. When you create Ink Annotations, they are saved with the presentation and are visible thereafter even by users who do not have or use Tablet PCs.

Ink Annotations can be particularly useful when you collaborate with a team on presentation content. You can add an Ink Annotation on a slide asking a team

member to investigate or research a topic. You can even sketch out how you want a slide to appear when finished to help the team member responsible for the slide.

There are several pen styles from which to choose, including Ballpoint, Felt Tip, and Highlighters. Each pen style gives the Ink Annotations a different shape or width. You can also choose from a variety of Ink colors, with the default colors coming from the slide's design theme.

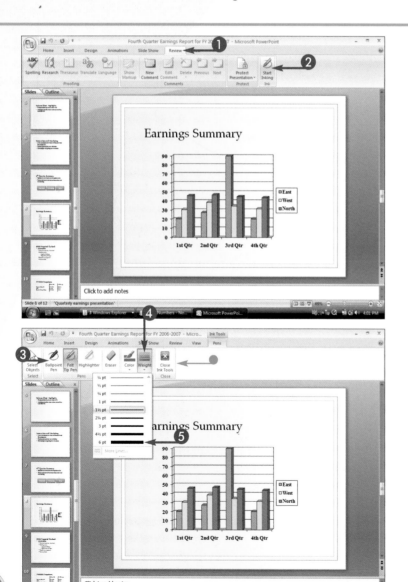

① Click the Review tab.

② Click Start Inking.

● The Ink Tools controls appear.

③ Click the pen style you want to use.

④ Click Weight.

⑤ Click the line width you want to use.

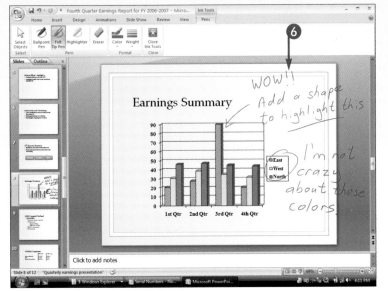

6 Ink the slide as desired.

7 Repeat Steps **3** to **6** to continue inking in a different pen style or color.

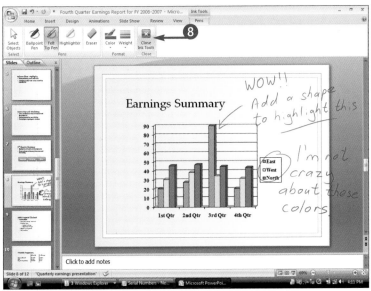

8 When you are finished, click Close Ink Tools.

The Ink stays on the slide.

TIPS

Try This!

To use ink annotations during presentations, position your Tablet PC input device pen over the lower part of the slide until you see the pen icon activated. Tap the pen icon and then use the menu that appears to tap the pen and color you want to use.

Customize It!

You can also use ink colors not included in the design theme you are using. Follow Steps **1** and **2** above to display the Ink Tools. Click Color and then click More Ink Colors. In the Colors dialog box, click the color you want to use. Click OK.

Reverse It!

You can erase ink annotations. To erase the most recent annotation, press Ctrl+Z. To erase any annotation, click the Eraser in the Pens tab, and then tap the annotation you want to erase.

Chapter 8

Expand Your Audience by Publishing to the Web

You can greatly expand your audience by publishing your presentations with Internet access. When you publish presentations to an intranet or Internet server, the presentations load as Web pages and are viewable even by those who do not have PowerPoint.

If you have access rights to a Web server, you can publish your presentation directly to the Internet, with no requirement for a separate Web publishing program. You can also use Web Page Preview to view how your presentation will look before you publish it to a Web site.

When a presentation is saved to the Web, the presentation's outline is used to create a list of hyperlinks to each slide to make it easy for

viewers to navigate to the slides in your presentation. You can specify the colors, the fonts, and even the page title that appears at the top of the page to make the Web presentation your own. You can also publish your presentation to an XPS or PDF file.

If you know the screen resolution at which viewers will have their monitors set, you can create your presentation to look custom-made for that screen resolution. You can even optimize your presentation to work best on a specific brand or version of browser. After your presentation is posted to the Web, you can easily link to it from text or graphics in another presentation.

Top 100

Turn your presentation into an
ONLINE RESOURCE

You can make your presentation widely available when you use the Save As command's Single File Web Page option. The Single File Web Page format allows users to double-click the file and then see a Web-based presentation that displays Outline, Notes, and Presentation panes. Viewers can easily navigate between all of the slides as well.

After you have used Save As to convert your presentation to the Single File Web Page format, you can post the resulting file on a file server, an

intranet, or Internet Web server for anyone to access and view. Users can double-click the file from an e-mail message or network location to open their browser and load the presentation. When users click a link to the presentation, they are prompted to open the presentation in their browser, or save it to their computer's hard drive. The ability to save the entire presentation to the hard drive makes the Single File Web Page format an attractive way to distribute your presentations.

1 Click the Office button.

2 Click Save As.

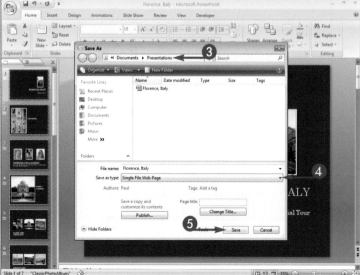

The Save As dialog box appears.

3 Navigate to the folder in which you want to save the online presentation.

4 Click Single File Web Page.

5 Click Save.

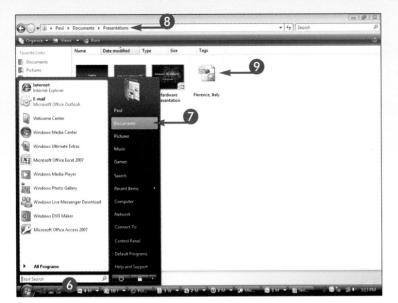

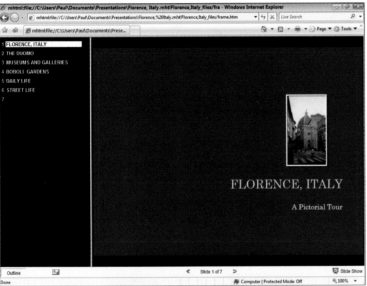

PowerPoint saves the presentation for use in a Web browser.

6 Click Start.

7 Click Documents.

Note: In Windows XP, click My Documents, instead.

8 Select the folder in which you saved your browser-based presentation.

9 Double-click the file to open it.

Your Web browser starts.

10 If you are using Internet Explorer, you may see the information pane telling you that it could not load "ActiveX controls." If so, click the pane, click Allow Blocked Content, and then click Yes.

The online presentation opens in the browser.

Note: To learn how to navigate a browser-based presentation, see Task #74.

#71

DIFFICULTY LEVEL

TIPS

Did You Know?

You can create HTML pages instead of Single File Web Pages. The HTML option creates a single Web page for each slide. To save a presentation as HTML, follow Steps **1** to **3** above, and then in Step **4** select Web Page. Proceed with Step **5**. A folder is created that contains the HTML pages and a separate graphics folder.

Change It!

You can change the title that appears in the browser's title bar. After Step **4**, click Change Title. In the Set Page Title dialog box, type the new page title in the Page title field. Click OK, and then proceed with Step **5**.

PUBLISH YOUR PRESENTATION
directly to a Web site

You can make your presentation available to anyone with an Internet browser when you use PowerPoint's Publish option. Publish allows you to send your online presentation directly to a Web server that supports the WebDAV standard, the FrontPage Server Extensions, SharePoint Team Services, or Windows SharePoint Services.

For example, instead of creating Single File Web Pages or HTML pages for your presentation and then using a Web site publishing or FTP program to

transfer the files to your Web server, you can use the Publish option. Publish allows you to specify a target server URL to which to publish, creates the necessary files, and then moves them to the Web server for you. This makes publishing to a Web server nearly as easy as saving a document.

After the presentation has been published to the Web server, it can be linked to any other Web page. Viewers see the Outline, Notes, and Presentation panes, and can easily navigate between slides.

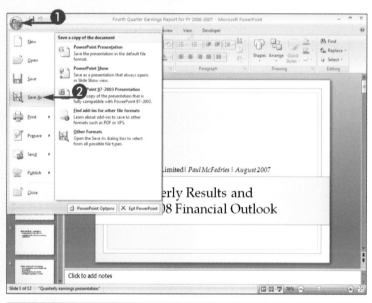

① Click the Office button.

② Click Save As.

The Save As dialog box appears.

③ Use the Save as type list to click either Single File Web Page or Web Page.

④ Click Publish.

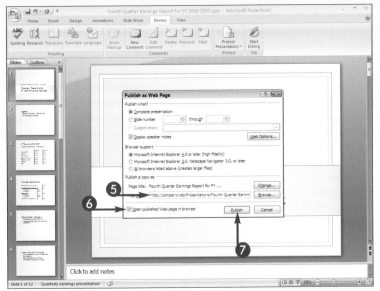

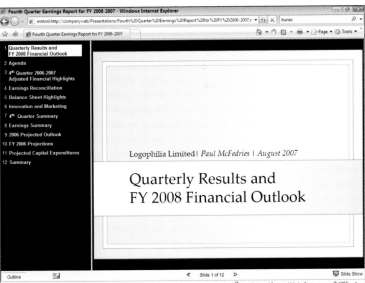

The Publish as Web Page dialog box appears.

⑤ Type the path to the Web server and the target file name in the File name text box.

⑥ Click the Open published Web page in browser option (☐ changes to ☑).

⑦ Click Publish.

Note: *You may receive a prompt to enter a user name and password in order to access the site.*

PowerPoint publishes the presentation to the Web server, and the browser opens with the presentation loaded.

Note: *To learn how to navigate a browser-based presentation, see Task #74.*

Caution!

You must have the proper security and permissions to access the Web server. A prompt will ask you to supply a valid user name and password before you can access the Web server.

Important!

The path in Step **5** is a combination of the Web site address and the file name. For example, if your Web site address is www.myserver. com, and the file name is myppt.mht, the path you would type is the following: **http://www.myserver.com/ myppt.mht**.

Did You Know?

You can save the presentation as an HTML page instead of a Single File Web Page. Follow Steps **1** and **2**; in the Save As dialog box, click the Save as type list, and then click Web Page. Proceed with Step **4**.

Publish your presentation to an
XPS OR PDF FILE

You can give yourself more publishing flexibility by publishing your presentation to a PDF or XPS file.

A browser-based presentation does not always look exactly the way it appears within the PowerPoint window. Internet Explorer generally does a good job of rendering the presentation, but other browsers may not. You will learn techniques later in this chapter that help you tweak the publishing of presentations to the Web, but these settings do not always work for all browsers.

If you want other people to see your slides exactly as you made them, consider forgoing Web pages and publishing your presentation as a PDF or XPS file. PDF stands for Portable Document Format and it is a standard format for representing documents exactly as they appeared originally. Most people have a PDF reader installed on their computer.

XPS stands for XML Paper Specification, and like PDF it renders a document exactly like the original. Internet Explorer 7 supports displaying XPS documents.

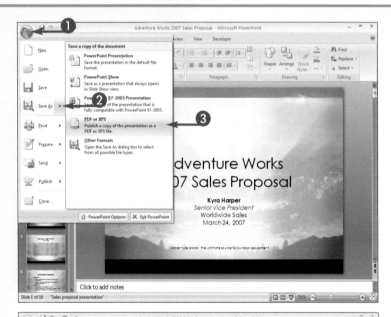

① Click the Office button.

② Click the Save As arrow.

③ Click PDF or XPS.

Note: If you do not see the PDF or XPS command, you must install the Publish as PDF or XPS add-in. See the Tips on the following page for the details.

The Publish as PDF or XPS dialog box appears.

④ Select the folder in which you want to save the file.

⑤ Click here and select either PDF or XPS Document.

6 If you chose XPS Document in Step **5**, click Open file after publishing (☐ changes to ☑).

7 Click Standard (◯ changes to ◉).

8 Click Publish.

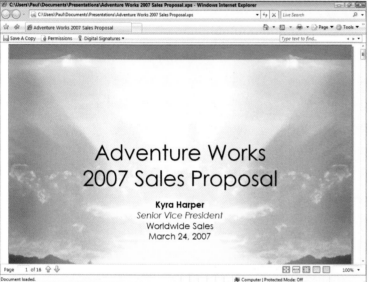

PowerPoint publishes the presentation to the PDF or XPS format.

If you published to an XPS file, Internet Explorer opens and displays the file.

More Options!

By default, PowerPoint publishes just the presentation's slides. However, you can also publish your presentation's handouts, notes pages, or outline view. Follow Steps **1** to **7** to set up your presentation for publishing. Click Options, use the Publish what list to click what you want to publish, click OK, and then proceed with Step **8**.

Try This!

Support for PDF and XPS files is not built into Microsoft Office 2007. Instead, you need to download and install an add-in file from Microsoft that adds the capability to publish to these formats to each Office application. Click Office, click the arrow beside Save As, click Find add-ins for other file formats, and then click the Microsoft Save as PDF or XPS Add-in for 2007 Microsoft Office programs link.

NAVIGATE A PRESENTATION
in a browser

When viewing a presentation in a Web browser, you can take advantage of the controls displayed by the browser to navigate the presentation.

When you save a presentation for the Web, you can view the resulting Single File Web Page file or HTML Web Page file in a Web browser. The Web presentation offers tools for moving from slide to slide. In most cases, you get arrow buttons to move forward and backward through the slides; you get an Outline pane that enables you to jump to a slide by

clicking it; you can toggle the Outline pane on and off; and you can expand and collapse the outline to show more or less detail. You can also start and stop narration and display the presentation in Full Screen mode.

Whether you saved a presentation to your hard disk or published it directly to a Web server, you should view your Web presentation immediately to make sure it looks and operates the way you want.

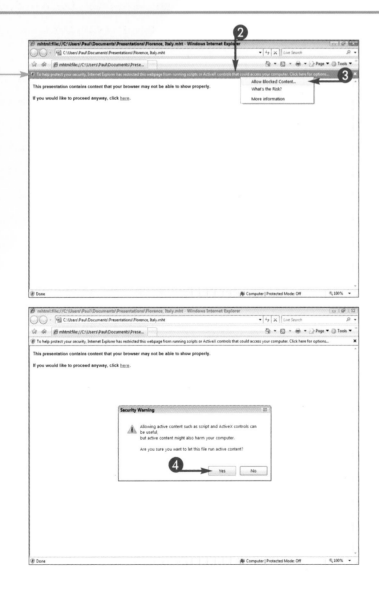

① If you saved the presentation to the hard disk, double-click the HTM or MHT file in a folder window on the Windows desktop. Or, if you've already published the presentation, open your Web browser and navigate to the address for the Web presentation.

● Internet Explorer displays the Information bar, which tells you the program is not displaying the ActiveX control that runs the browser-based presentation.

② Click the Information bar.

③ Click Allow Blocked Content.

The Security Warning dialog box appears.

④ Click Yes.

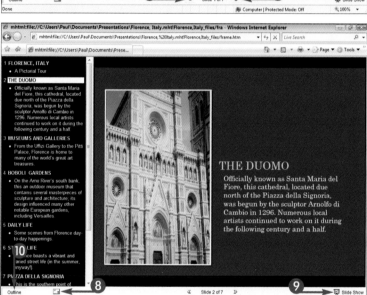

The presentation appears in the browser window.

⑤ Click the Next Slide arrow to move forward one slide at a time.

⑥ Click the Previous Slide arrow to move backward one slide at a time.

⑦ Click a slide title in the Outline pane to navigate to that slide.

#74

DIFFICULTY LEVEL

⑧ Click Expand/Collapse Outline to show more or less of the presentation outline.

⑨ Click Slide Show to display the presentation in Full Screen Slide Show format.

⑩ Click Outline to toggle the outline on and off.

TIPS

Did You Know?

When you click Slide Show, Internet Explorer must load a different ActiveX control to display the presentation in Full Screen Slide Show mode. By default, Internet Explorer also blocks this control, which means that you once again see the Information bar. Click the bar, click Allow Blocked Content, and then click Yes.

Try This!

In the Full Screen Slide Show mode, you navigate to the next slide by clicking anywhere on the screen. If you want to return to the previous slide, right-click the screen and then click Previous. To return to the regular presentation viewing mode, either right-click the screen and then click End Show, or press Esc.

Specify the
DEFAULT FONTS
for Web-based presentations

You can control how your online presentation looks by changing the default fonts. Presentations often use fonts that are installed when PowerPoint is installed, but the same fonts may not be available on the systems viewers use to access a presentation online.

As part of the publishing process, you can specify default fonts used in Web presentations. You can specify proportional fonts and fixed-width fonts. Proportional fonts allow each character to take up a different amount of space. For example, a letter *i* would be narrower than a letter *w* in a proportional

font. Fixed-width fonts dedicate the same amount of space for every character.

You can specify proportional and fixed-width fonts. Most browsers specify the use of default proportional fonts (Web page fonts) and fixed-width fonts (plain text fonts) when fonts are not specified on Web pages, or when the specified fonts are not available. By specifying the default fonts for a Web-based presentation, you can control the fonts that your audience sees when they view your presentation on the Web.

① Click the Office button.

② Click PowerPoint Options.

The PowerPoint Options dialog box appears.

③ Click Advanced

④ Click Web Options.

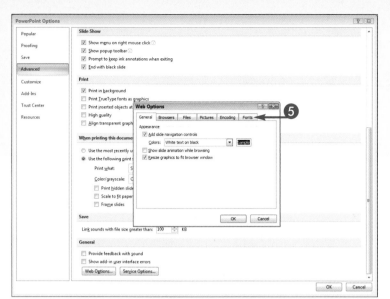

The Web Options dialog box appears.

⑤ Click the Fonts tab.

#75

DIFFICULTY LEVEL

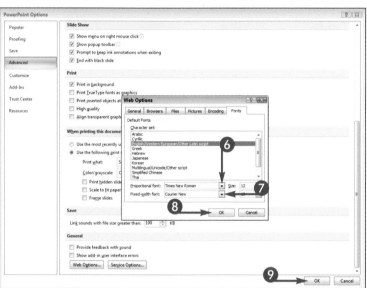

⑥ Click here and select the proportional font you want to use.

⑦ Click here and select the fixed-width font you want to use.

⑧ Click OK.

⑨ Click OK.

PowerPoint uses the new fonts in all future browser-based presentations that you publish.

TIPS

Did You Know?
You can specify the default proportional font size. Follow Steps **1** to **6** above, and then use the Size list to the right of the Proportional font list to click the default proportional font size.

Did You Know!
You can specify the default fixed-width font size. Follow Steps **1** to **7** above, and then use the Size list to the right of the Fixed-width font list to click the default fixed-width font size.

Go International!
You can specify the default character set when you create presentations for an international audience. Follow Steps **1** to **5** above. In the Character set section, scroll up or down to locate the character set you want to use, and then click to select it. Proceed with Step **6**.

CUSTOMIZE COLORS
in Web-based presentations

You can customize the colors used in Web-based presentations to suit your tastes. By default, the Outline and Notes panes in online presentations have a black background with white fonts. Similarly, the area behind the slide is black. However, you can publish your presentations using colors that coordinate with your presentation's look and feel instead of using the default black.

You can change Web presentation colors as part of PowerPoint's Web options. When you use the Presentation colors (accent color) option, PowerPoint uses the default colors and primary font color from

the design theme that is applied to your presentation. For example, if you use the Foundry theme colors, which are mostly green, you may want the Outline, Notes, and Presentation panes to use the same green colors as well.

After preferences have been changed to match the presentation's colors, when the presentation is published to a Web format, the presentation blends in with the Outline, Notes, and Presentation panes. Coordination of the background colors makes for a more polished and professional-looking online presentation.

① Click the Office button.

② Click PowerPoint Options.

The PowerPoint Options dialog box appears.

③ Click Advanced

④ Click Web Options.

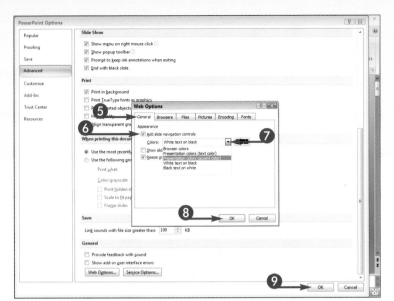

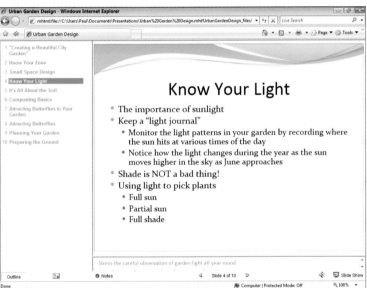

The Web Options dialog box appears.

5 Click the General tab.

6 Click the Add slide navigation controls option (☐ changes to ☑).

7 Click here and select the color option you want.

8 Click OK.

9 Click OK.

10 Publish the presentation as described in Tasks #71 and 72.

The presentation is published with a Web interface that uses your color selections.

TIPS

Caution!

You can change the default background color to the default background color of the viewer's browser. Simply follow the steps above, but in Step **7** click Browser colors instead of Presentation colors (accent color). However, results will be unpredictable.

Did You Know?

You can change the default black background with white text to white background with black text. Follow the steps above, but in Step **7** click Black text on white instead of Presentation colors (accent color).

Did You Know?

You can use the design theme's text color instead of using the design theme's accent color. Follow the steps above, but in Step **7** click Presentation colors (text color) instead of Presentation colors (accent color).

CHANGE THE TITLE
for a Web-based presentation

You can change text that appears at the top of a viewer's Web browser when you create online presentations by changing the title bar text. The title bar appears at the top of the browser window, and helps users identify the page that they are viewing. Note, too, that title text also appears in the tab for programs that support tabbed browsing.

Page titles should be descriptive enough to give viewers context for what page they are on, but not so long that that they take effort to read. Most Web site visitors glance quickly at page titles to make

sure that they are on the right page, but do not spend time studying them.

Page titles can draw attention to important messages. For example, if your presentation is promoting a new product or service, you can include special characters, such as *!*, ***, or *#* in the page title to draw attention to it or include information about the sale in the page title. Because this information appears in the user's browser, it is another good way to communicate a message to viewers of your online presentation.

① Click the Office button.

② Click Save As.

The Save As dialog box appears.

③ Select the folder in which you want to save the online presentation.

④ Click here and select either Single File Web Page or Web Page.

⑤ Click Change Title.

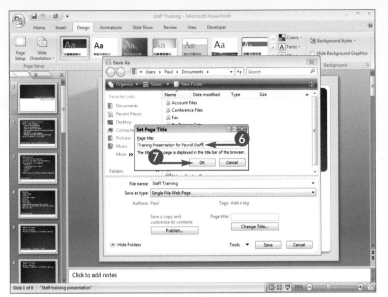

The Set Page Title dialog box appears.

⑥ Type the page title.

⑦ Click OK.

The Set Page Title dialog box closes.

⑧ To continue publishing, follow Steps **4** to **10** in Task #71.

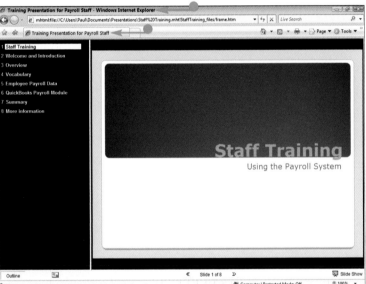

● PowerPoint publishes the presentation with the specified title on the browser title bar and in the current tab.

TIPS

Did You Know?
Page titles are also used when viewers switch from program to program by pressing Alt+Tab. Text length is limited in the program switching dialog box, so you should make sure that page titles are not too long.

Try This!
If you have multiple browser windows open and then click the Windows taskbar to see what browser window you want to switch to, the page title appears. This space is limited, so be sure to limit page title length.

Did You Know?
Because some Internet search engines use page titles to help users search for Web content, use page titles that utilize key words by which users may search.

Change the target
SCREEN RESOLUTION
for Web-based presentations

You can optimize your presentation for a specific screen resolution to give it the best possible appearance. When you publish your presentation online, it is often difficult to anticipate the size at which viewers will have their screens set. One user may have an older monitor that is set at a smaller size of 640 pixels wide by 480 pixels high. Another may have a newer, larger monitor that is set at 1024 x 768.

However, today's corporate users are likely to have similar hardware and screen resolutions. When you

know that users have newer monitors, for example, you can predict that most will view presentations at 800 x 600 or 1024 x 768. Therefore, you can set PowerPoint to publish online presentations in a format that looks best at those screen resolutions.

You can also set the screen resolution to work best on smaller screens, such as those used on notebook or handheld devices. For example, a presentation for a sales force using handheld devices could be optimized for 544 x 376.

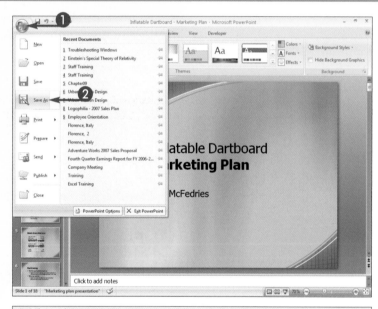

① Click the Office button.

② Click Save As.

The Save As dialog box appears.

③ Navigate to the folder in which you want to save the online presentation.

④ Click here and select either Single File Web Page or Web Page.

⑤ Click Publish.

DIFFICULTY LEVEL

The Publish as Web Page dialog box appears.

⑥ Click Web Options.

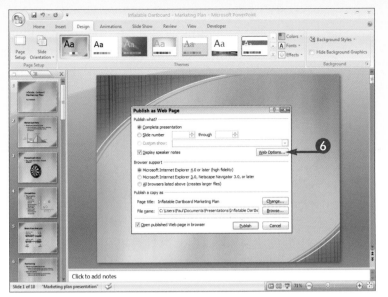

The Web Options dialog box appears.

⑦ Click the Pictures tab.

⑧ Click here and select the resolution you want.

⑨ Click OK.

⑩ Click Publish.

PowerPoint publishes the presentation optimized for the screen size you selected.

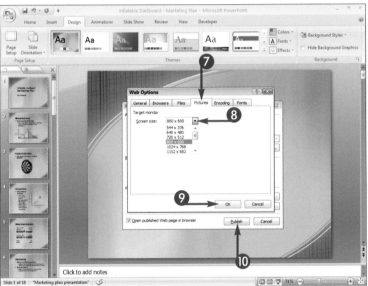

TIPS

Include It!

You can optimize the screen resolution when you want to display the content of a frame in another browser window. For example, if you publish at a smaller screen resolution, you can bring the presentation into another Web page and still have room for additional content.

Did You Know?

You can change the default optimum screen size that PowerPoint uses for all of your presentations. Click Office and then click PowerPoint Options to open the PowerPoint Options dialog box. Click Advanced and then click Web Options to open the Web Options dialog box. Follow Steps **7** to **10** in this task to set the resolution, and then click OK.

OPTIMIZE YOUR PRESENTATION
for a specific browser

You can help assure that your online presentation is accessible by users with the most popular browsers when you optimize your presentation for specific browsers. You can accomplish this by selecting browser brands and versions that you want to make sure your presentation works well with.

Options include Microsoft Internet Explorer 3.0 or later and Netscape Navigator 3.0 or later. Default Web presentations are optimized for Microsoft Internet Explorer 4.0 or later because the majority of Internet browsers fall in this category. However, if

you are creating a presentation for use within your company and your company is standardized on Microsoft Office 2007 programs like PowerPoint 2007, you can instead choose to create presentations for Internet Explorer 6.0 or later because Office 2007 supports it. Conversely, if you are creating a Web presentation for use on the Internet, you may want to optimize your presentation for both Internet Explorer 4.0 and Netscape Navigator 4.0 or later to make your presentation viewable by a broad array of users with a variety of Web browsers.

1 Click the Office button.

2 Click Save As.

The Save As dialog box appears.

3 Navigate to the folder in which you want to save the online presentation.

4 Click here and select either Single File Web Page or Web Page.

5 Click Publish.

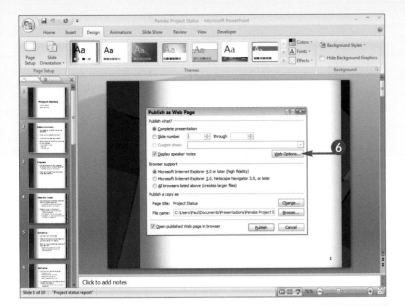

The Publish as Web Page dialog box appears.

6 Click Web Options.

DIFFICULTY LEVEL

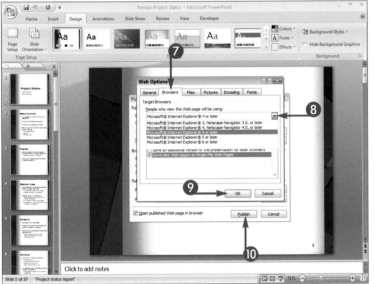

The Web Options dialog box appears.

7 Click the Browsers tab.

8 Click here and select the browser you want to use.

9 Click OK.

10 Click Publish.

The presentation is published optimized for the chosen browser or browser combination.

TIPS

Caution!

Online presentation files get larger as more browser brands and versions are supported because additional code is necessary to support features in older browsers. Be conservative in the range of browsers for which you choose to optimize your presentation. Optimizing your presentation for Internet Explorer 6.0 creates the smallest and fastest-to-load file size. Conversely, presentations optimized for Internet Explorer 3.0 and Netscape Navigator 3.0 or later create larger files that load more slowly.

Caution!

Not all features in your presentation work on all browser brands and versions. For example, some slide transitions and animations do not work on older browser versions.

LINK YOUR PRESENTATION
to another Web page

You can leverage your presentation by publishing it to a Web server and then linking to it from another presentation. For example, if you publish a presentation about your products to the Internet, you could link to it from a presentation about your company's marketing efforts.

The key to successfully linking to an online presentation is browsing to it, and then creating the hyperlink to it. When you publish an online presentation as a Single File Web Page, you are publishing to a path such as

www.server.com/filename.mht, but when it is viewed in the browser, it resolves to an address of mhtml:http://www.server.com/filename.mht!filename _files/frame.htm. You can link to the resolved address to make the presentation load as quickly as possible.

When you create a hyperlink to an online presentation, you can browse to the presentation to which you want to link, after which you are returned to the presentation to complete the steps for creating the hyperlink.

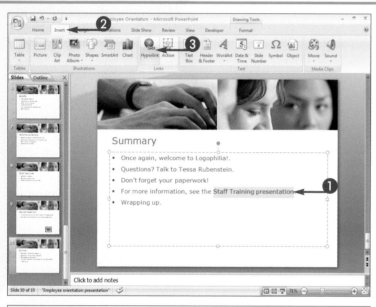

① Select the text to which you want to apply a hyperlink.

② Click the Insert tab.

③ Click Hyperlink.

The Insert Hyperlink dialog box appears.

④ Click Existing File or Web Page.

⑤ Click the Browse the Web button.

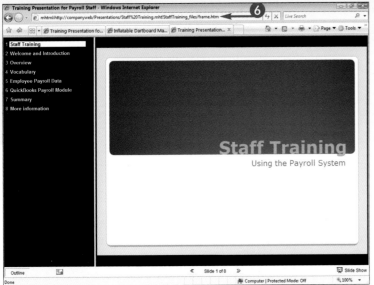

The browser opens.

6 Browse to the presentation to which you want to link.

7 Press Alt+Tab to return to PowerPoint.

80

DIFFICULTY LEVEL

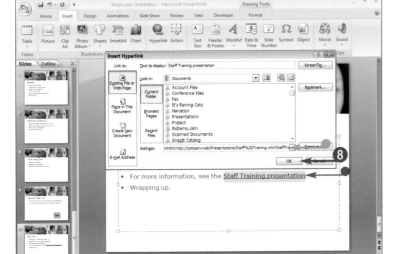

● The address appears in the Address text box.

8 Click OK.

● PowerPoint inserts the hyperlink into your presentation text.

TIPS

Try This!
You can create a hyperlink from a picture or a shape. In Step **1** above, click the picture or shape instead of highlighting text, and then proceed with Step **2**.

Try This!
You can create a hyperlink to a presentation that is located on a file share. Follow Steps **1** to **3** above, and then click the Browse for File button instead of the Browse the Web button.

Try This!
You can specify text to appear when you position your mouse pointer over a hyperlink. Follow Steps **1** to **4** above, and then click ScreenTip. In the Set Hyperlink ScreenTip dialog box, type the ScreenTip text. Click OK, and then proceed with Step **5** above.

Collaborate with Others

You can enlist the help of others in reviewing or editing your presentations when you use collaboration features. You can safeguard your presentation by requiring a password in order to view it. You can send presentations to others in e-mail messages to review, and when they are finished editing the presentations, they can easily return them to you. Reviewers' edits are easy to identify and then act upon, and you can even consolidate multiple versions of your presentation and see who made each change to it. You can also use comments to add notes to presentations without changing the content itself.

You can also send presentations to others for review as shared attachments. Shared attachments are stored on a central Web server running Windows SharePoint Services as a shared workspace. When users receive your presentation in an e-mail message, they are prompted to check to see if there is a more current version on the shared workspace, which assures that each user is working with the latest version of your presentation.

You can access and modify resources on your shared workspace from within PowerPoint. You can use your shared workspace to view document version information. You can even sign up to receive an e-mail message when anything on your shared workspace changes.

Top 100

Safeguard your presentation with a
PASSWORD

You can keep your presentation from being opened by unauthorized users when you assign a password to it. Passwords are a combination of characters that the user must type correctly before performing an action.

You can require one password for opening a presentation and another for editing a presentation. For example, if your presentation includes confidential sales information, you could require a password in order to open it. Similarly, if you have a presentation you want certain users to be able to make changes

to and then save, you can create another password for the right to make changes to the presentation and then save them.

When users open a presentation that you have open- and edit-password protected, they are prompted for the password to open the presentation and then for a password to edit the presentation. If they do not have the edit password, they can open the presentation in read-only mode, which allows them to see the presentation but not make changes to it.

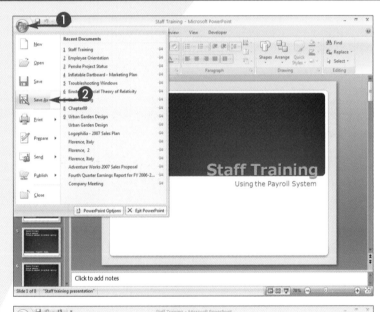

① Click the Office button.

② Click Save As.

The Save As dialog box appears.

③ Click Tools.

④ Click General Options.

The General Options dialog box appears.

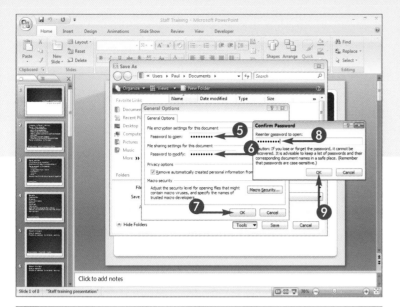

⑤ Type the opening password.

⑥ Type the modifying password.

⑦ Click OK.

The Confirm Password dialog box appears.

⑧ Retype the password for opening presentations.

⑨ Click OK to confirm the password for opening the presentation.

81

DIFFICULTY LEVEL

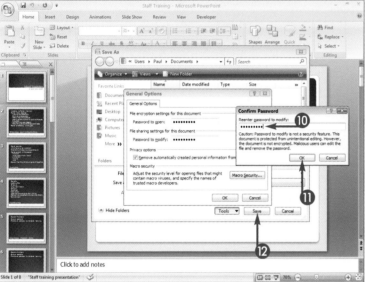

The Confirm Password dialog box appears.

⑩ Retype the password for modifying presentations.

⑪ Click OK to confirm the password for editing the presentation.

⑫ Click Save.

The Confirm Save As dialog box appears.

⑬ Click Yes.

PowerPoint sets the passwords for opening and modifying the presentation.

TIPS

Caution!
Users can share passwords with others. For example, if you send the presentation attached to an e-mail message and include the password in the message body, the user can easily forward the message to someone else.

Caution!
Users who have only the password required to open a presentation can still use Save As to save the presentation to another file.

Important!
If you are going to require passwords for accessing your presentations, you should use strong passwords. Strong passwords use combinations of lower- and uppercase letters, numbers, and special symbols to make it more difficult for people to guess the password. For example, 4Apple$ is considered a strong password, while 4apples is not.

Use comments to
ADD NOTES

You can use comments as a way to communicate with reviewers or insert a reminder into a slide. Comments are like electronic sticky notes that you can use to type any text you want.

Comments can be a great way to communicate with a presentation's author without changing the presentation itself. For example, if you want to remind the presentation's author to insert a new slide or do some additional research, changing the presentation content might not be an appropriate

way to do it. Instead, you can insert a comment as a highly visible way to get the author's attention.

Comments inserted into a slide appear with a different color for each reviewer. They also display the name of the reviewer who made the comment and the date the comment was inserted or edited. When the comments are not opened, a small colored box appears that shows the initials of the person who inserted the comment plus a number. This enables one person to insert more than one comment on a page, such as PM1, PM2, and PM3.

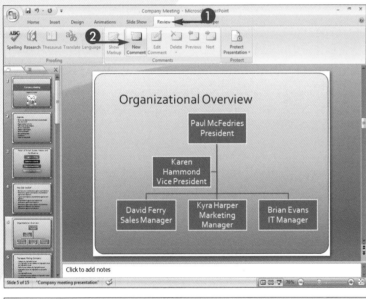

INSERT A NEW COMMENT

① Click the Review tab.

② Click New Comment.

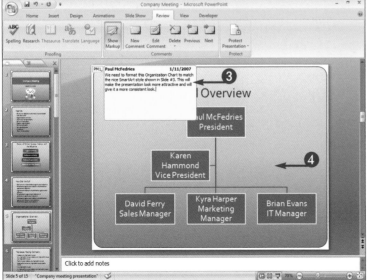

A blank comment is inserted into the slide.

③ Click the comment form, and then type your comments.

④ Click off the comment on the slide.

The comment form closes but the comment symbol remains.

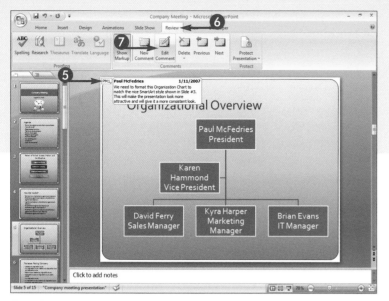

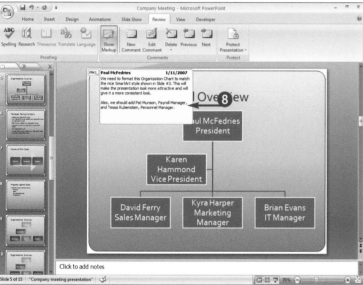

⑤ Click the comment symbol.

⑥ Click Review.

⑦ Click Edit Comment.

82

DIFFICULTY LEVEL

The comment form appears.

⑧ Click and then type to edit the comment.

TIPS

Name It!

You can change the name and initials that appear in comments. Click Office, and then PowerPoint Options. Click Popular, change the name in the User name text box, and then the initials in the Initials text box. Click OK. Future comments will use the new name and initials.

Move It!

You can move a comment on a slide by clicking and dragging it to a new location.

Caution!

If another reviewer edits your comment, it will show that reviewer's name and initials, not yours. Similarly, if you edit another person's comment, it will look like your comment. Therefore, consider editing your own comments, but add new comments instead of editing the comments of others.

Send your presentation as an
E-MAIL ATTACHMENT

You can send your presentation to others as an e-mail attachment. When you send a presentation as an e-mail attachment, your e-mail client opens with a new message with your presentation attached that is ready to address and then send.

By sending presentations as e-mail attachments, you can save time. Instead of finding a network location that all recipients have access to and then sending an e-mail message requesting updates to the presentation, you can instead just send the presentation via e-mail. When you send a presentation

as an attachment, you can look up recipients in your e-mail address book.

It also saves time to use PowerPoint's Send E-mail command because it creates the e-mail message and attaches the presentation to it automatically. Without this command, you would have to open Microsoft Outlook, start a new e-mail message, run the insert attachment command, and then find the presentation that you want to send. These steps are taken care of when you use PowerPoint's Send E-mail command.

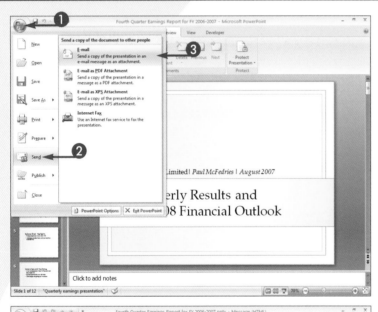

❶ Click the Office button.

❷ Click Send.

❸ Click E-mail.

Microsoft Outlook opens with a new mail message created and the presentation attached.

❹ Click To.

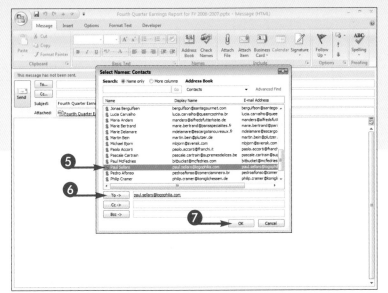

The Select Names: Contacts dialog box appears.

⑤ Click the name of the person to whom you want to send the presentation.

Note: If you want to send to more than one person, Ctrl-click to select more than one name.

DIFFICULTY LEVEL

⑥ Click To.

⑦ Click OK.

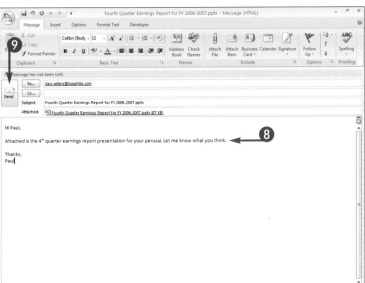

⑧ Type your message in the body of the e-mail.

⑨ Click Send.

The message is sent with the presentation attached.

TIPS

Caution!

You should use caution when you use e-mail to send large presentations. Some recipients may use e-mail providers that limit the size of attachments. Additionally, users with low bandwidth connections may not want to wait for large presentations to download when they check for e-mail.

Did You Know?

You can type the complete e-mail addresses of the people to whom you want to send the e-mail message instead of looking them up in your address book. In Step **4** above, type the e-mail addresses, separated by semicolons, on the To line. You can then omit Steps **5** to **7** above. If those users are in your address book, their display names will appear.

Collaborate by saving a presentation to a
SHAREPOINT SITE

You can collaborate with network users by placing the presentation in a shared network folder and giving those users access to the folder. However, what if you want to work with people who do not have access to your network? These days, many businesses are "virtual" in the sense that they consist of permanent employees and temporary contract workers, all of whom work or live in separate locations. For these far-flung businesses, you can still use Exchange Server via a hosting service, but this usually means creating a separate Outlook profile just for the Exchange Server account,

which is a hassle if you also have POP or HTTP accounts, for example.

A better solution for many businesses is a Web site that runs Windows SharePoint Services, an extension to Windows Server that enables users to come together online as a virtual "team" for sharing documents, lists, calendars, and contacts, and to have online discussions and meetings. The most basic form of collaboration on a SharePoint site is to save a file in a document library, which is a folder on the site that stores documents added by team members.

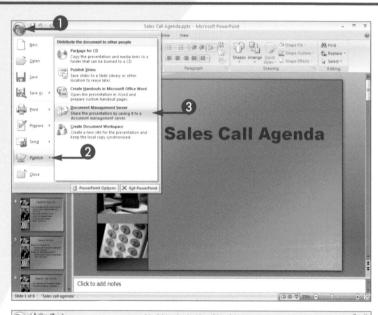

① Click the Office button.

② Click Publish.

③ Click Document Management Server.

The Save As dialog box appears.

④ Click the Address bar icon.

⑤ Delete the existing address and type the address of your SharePoint server.

⑥ Click Go To.

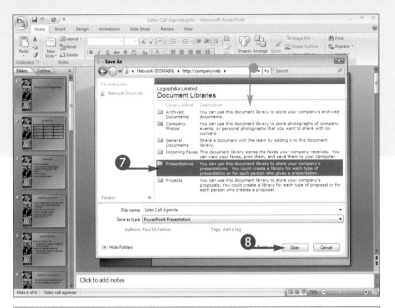

- A list of document libraries appears.

(7) Click the document library you want to use.

(8) Click Open.

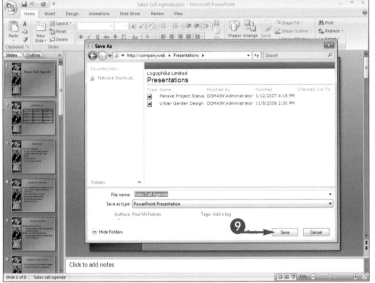

The contents of the document library appear.

(9) Click Save.

PowerPoint saves a copy of the presentation in the document library.

TIPS

Try This!

If you want to work with a presentation that has been stored in a SharePoint document library, click Office and then click Open. In the Open dialog box, follow Steps **4** to **8** in this task to open the document library that contains the presentation. Click the presentation and then click Open.

Did You Know?

Other people who have access to the SharePoint site can also work on the presentation that you saved to the document library. If you want to work on the presentation exclusively, open it as described in the previous tip. Click the Office button, click Server, and then click Check Out. When you are done, click the Check In link in the Document Management task pane.

Collaborate on presentations with a
DOCUMENT WORKSPACE

You can create a document workspace that team members can use for centralized storage and as a collaboration location. Document workspaces are Web sites that are provisioned for you to store documents and document information, lists of links, lists of team members, and tasks. Document workspaces rely on Windows Server and Windows SharePoint Services, and you must have access rights in order to create document workspaces. Document workspaces make it easy for you to work with others on your presentation because reviewers are assured that the presentations that they open are the most recent versions.

The Document Management task pane gives you a view of each document workspace without leaving PowerPoint to go to your browser. Creating a new document workspace from the Document Management task pane creates the document workspace on the server, and then includes a hyperlink to workspace in the Document Management task pane. You can add members, documents, tasks, and links to the document workspace from the Document Management task pane in PowerPoint or from the browser.

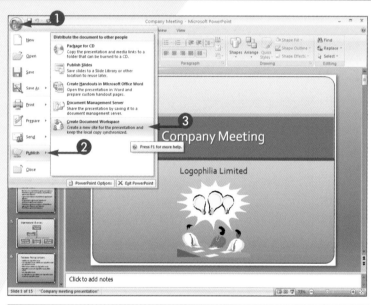

① Click the Office button.

② Click Publish.

③ Click Create Document Workspace.

The Document Management task pane appears.

④ Edit the name of the document workspace, as needed.

⑤ Type the address of the Web site in which you want to create the document workspace.

⑥ Click Create.

188

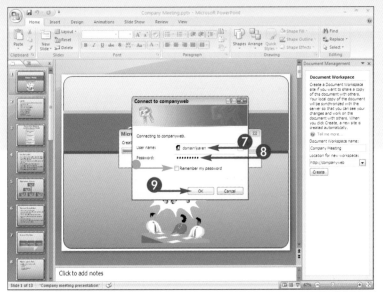

The Connect dialog box appears.

7 Type your user name for the SharePoint site.

8 Type your password for the SharePoint site.

● If you want to avoid the Connect dialog box in the future, click Remember my password (☐ changes to ☑).

9 Click OK.

10 If the Connect dialog box reappears, repeat Steps **7** to **9**.

The Document Workspace is provisioned for you and reflected in the Document Management task pane.

TIPS

More Options!

You can also make changes to your document workspace from the browser. To access the document workspace in the browser, click the Open site in browser link in the Document Management task pane to open the document workspace in the browser.

Did You Know?

The presentation filename is the default name given to a document workspace. For example, a presentation called budget.pptx would be saved to a document workspace at http://<*yoursite*>/budget/.

Did You Know?

When you are not using the Document Management task pane, you can click the Close button (X) to remove the task pane and give your presentation more room. To redisplay the task pane, click Office, click Server, and then click Document Management Information.

ADD RELATED DOCUMENTS
to a document workspace

You can use a document workspace to keep all related documents in one place. This enables other workspace members to access not only the main document, but also other documents that contain related information.

For example, if you have already created a presentation on budget plans for the next year and have stored it on a document workspace, you may also want to store a budget spreadsheet or policy document there as well. This allows all team members who currently have access to the document workspace to also

access the additional documents you upload. This can be much more convenient than creating a separate document workspace for every document with which you and your team work.

You can add documents to an existing document workspace by first opening the presentation that is already stored in the document workspace to which you want to add documents. When that presentation opens, the Document Management task pane appears and displays the contents of the document workspace. You can then upload additional documents.

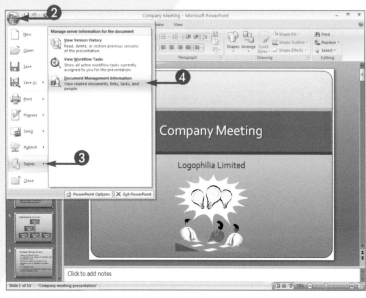

① Open the presentation that is stored in the document workspace.

Note: If PowerPoint asks whether you want to get the latest version from the document workspace, click Get Updates.

② Click the Office button.

③ Click Server.

④ Click Document Management Information.

Note: If you see the Connect dialog box, type your user name and password and click OK.

The Document Management task pane appears.

⑤ Click the Documents button.

⑥ Click Add new document.

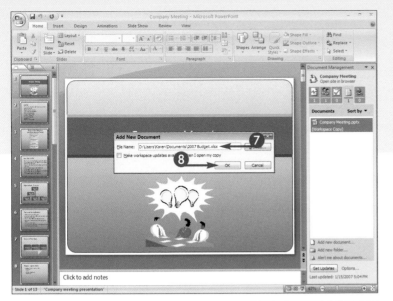

The Add New Document dialog box appears.

⑦ Type the path to the file that you want to upload to the document workspace.

⑧ Click OK.

 # 86

DIFFICULTY LEVEL

PowerPoint uploads the presentation to the document workspace.

● The presentation appears in the Documents list.

More Options!

You can also browse to a file to upload it instead of typing a path. Follow the steps above, but in Step **7**, click the Browse button. The Choose file dialog box appears. Navigate to the folder that contains the document. Click the file you want to add to the document workspace, click Open, and then proceed with Step **8**.

Did You Know?

Team members can also upload documents to the document workspace using their browsers. The easiest way to access it is to open a presentation that is stored in the document workspace, and then click the Open site in the browser link on the Document Management task pane.

CHANGE TEAM MEMBERS
in a document workspace

You can change who has access to a document workspace in which your presentation is stored without leaving PowerPoint. Because each document workspace is a Web site, making sure that team members have access rights is essential.

When you add team members to a document workspace, they can be added by their user name, Windows domain and user name, or by e-mail address. However, if you enter users by their e-mail address, they must also have a Windows account on the server running the document workspace. You must also decide what permission level to give to each new

member. A Reader can only view the presentation; a Contributor can add new content to the workspace; a Web Designer can create new document libraries and customize the site; and an Administrator has full control of the workspace.

After you have added new team members to the document workspace, their names appear on the Members tab in the Document Management task pane. You are also presented with a dialog box that asks if you want to send an e-mail message inviting new members to participate in the document workspace.

① Open the presentation that is stored in the document workspace.

Note: If PowerPoint asks whether you want to get the latest version from the document workspace, click Get Updates.

② Click the Members button.

Note: If you do not see the Document Management task pane, click Office, click Server, and then click Document Management Information.

③ Click Add new members.

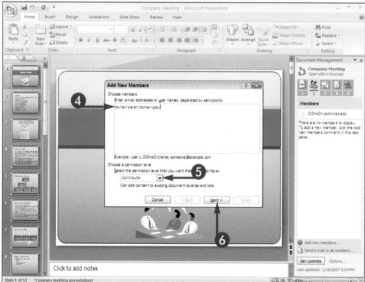

The Add New Members dialog box appears.

④ Type the e-mail addresses or Windows domain and user names.

Note: If you have multiple users to add, separate them with semicolons.

⑤ Use this list to click the permission level for the new members.

⑥ Click Next.

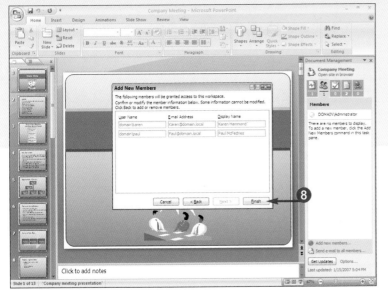

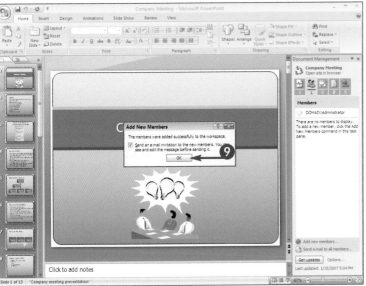

The next Add New Members dialog box appears.

⑦ Verify that the user names, e-mail addresses, and display names are the way you want them. If not, click Back and make the desired changes.

Note: *This is your last chance to change this information before adding it to the Web site.*

⑧ Click Finish.

DIFFICULTY LEVEL

The next Add New Members dialog box appears.

⑨ Click OK.

New members are sent an e-mail message welcoming them to the document workspace, and they are listed in the Document Management task pane.

TIPS

Did You Know?

You can also add new members from the document workspace on the SharePoint site. In the Document Management task pane, click Open site in the browser to view the workspace. On the Home page, click the Add new members link in the Members section. Follow the screens that appear.

More Options!

If you want to make changes to a member, click Members in the Document Management task pane. Click the drop-down arrow beside a member's name to display a list of actions. For example, you can click Send Mail to send the member a message, or you can click Edit Permission Level to change the member's workspace permissions.

Track your
PRESENTATION HISTORY

When you save a presentation to a document workspace, version information is automatically saved with it, such as the date and time when each version was saved, who saved each version, and the size of each version.

Version history is especially useful when you are responsible for presentations that are being edited by multiple users. The ability to find out who modified each version of the presentation makes each team member accountable and helps give you confidence in delegating presentation work to others.

Version information is accessible from the View Version History command on the Server menu. Each time a presentation is saved, a copy of that version is saved on the server, and information about that version is listed on the Versions dialog box. Version information displayed includes version number, date modified, who modified it, the size, and comments. When multiple versions are listed, you can click any of the versions and then restore that version or even delete it.

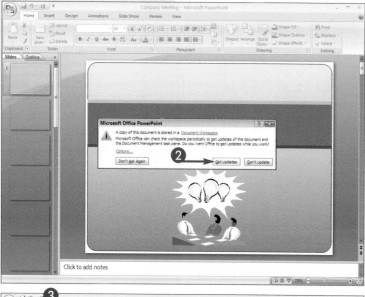

① Open the presentation whose revision history you want to check.

The Microsoft Office PowerPoint dialog box appears.

② Click Get Updates.

PowerPoint downloads the most recent version of the presentation.

③ Click the Office button.

④ Click Server.

⑤ Click View Version History.

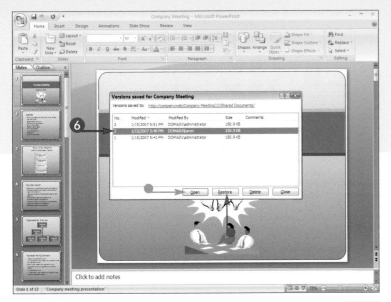

The Versions saved dialog box appears.

⑥ Click the version you want to work with.

● If you want to open that version, click Open.

● If you want to replace the current version of the presentation with the selected version, click Restore.

DIFFICULTY LEVEL

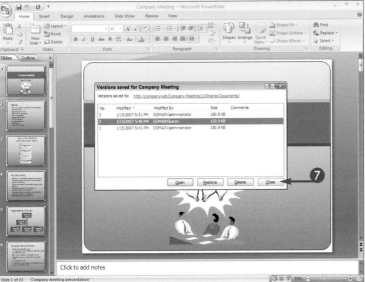

⑦ Click Close.

TIPS

Caution!
Versioning is very useful if your documents are important and you need the ability to roll back a presentation to a previous version. However, because a copy of each version is saved every time the presentation is saved, it means that each version takes up more hard disk space on your server. Therefore, you might want to routinely delete versions that you no longer need to keep. You can delete unneeded versions by following Steps **1** to **5** above, and then clicking Delete.

Caution!
When you delete a presentation, all versions of the presentation are deleted. Therefore, you should make sure that you do not need any backup versions of your presentations before you delete them.

Stay current when you
SUBSCRIBE TO ALERTS

You can stay updated on documents in your document workspace when you request alerts. Normally, when you save presentations to document workspaces, team members can get the most current version of the presentation whenever needed.

However, when you are anxiously awaiting feedback from team members on a presentation, it is tempting to continually check the document workspace for updates. This can waste quite a bit of your time if you repeatedly find that no updates are available. Instead, you can request an alert, which is an e-mail

message that is automatically generated from the server, telling you that your document has changed.

You can choose to receive an e-mail alert when anything changes in the document workspace. You can also specify how often you would like to receive alerts, such as weekly, daily, or directly after the document workspace changes. When you sign up for alerts, you are sent a confirmation e-mail message that contains a link to the document workspace, as well as a link to the alerts administration page.

① Open the presentation that is stored in the document workspace.

Note: *If PowerPoint asks whether you want to get the latest version from the document workspace, click Get Updates.*

② Click the Office button.

③ Click Server.

④ Click Document Management Information.

Note: *If you see the Connect dialog box, type your user name and password and click OK.*

The Document Management task pane appears.

⑤ Click the Documents button.

⑥ Click Alert me about documents.

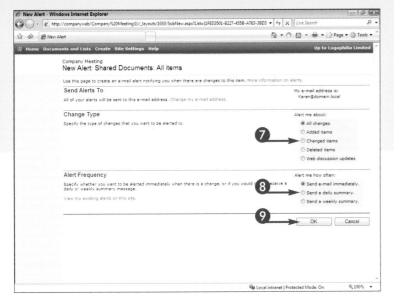

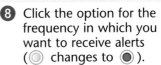

The browser opens to the New Alert page on the document workspace Web site.

⑦ Click the option for the type of changes to which you want to receive alerts (⊙ changes to ⦿).

DIFFICULTY LEVEL

⑧ Click the option for the frequency in which you want to receive alerts (⊙ changes to ⦿).

⑨ Click OK.

Your request for alerts is accepted, and you are automatically sent a confirmation e-mail message.

TIPS

Caution!

When users are removed from the document workspace, their alerts subscriptions stay in effect. To protect the security and privacy of your document workspace, when you remove users you should also remove their alerts subscriptions.

Caution!

Document workspaces that experience frequent use and continual updates may result in many e-mail alerts if you subscribe to receive them immediately. Busy sites with many updates may warrant daily updates instead.

Save It!

The confirmation e-mail message you receive after signing up for alerts contains a link to the alerts administration page. This link is also sent in alert e-mail messages in case you want to change the frequency of alerts or even cancel your alerts subscription.

ADD RELATED LINKS
to a document workspace

You can keep important information in one convenient location when you add related links to a document workspace. Document workspaces are displayed in PowerPoint on the Document Management task pane. The Links tab, also displayed on the Document Management task pane, enables you to add hyperlinks to direct document workspace users to related Web sites and documents stored on your company's network.

For example, in a document workspace created for a presentation about a new product, you could include hyperlinks to the product's marketing plan, to the product's Web site, and to a competitor's Web site, all from within the Document Management task pane. Anything that you can link to from a browser can be linked to from the Document Management task pane. When the visitor clicks one of the links, either the visitor's browser opens or the document or program linked to is launched.

For each link, you can specify a short description that appears in the Links tab, as well as a longer note that describes the link. This note appears when the user hovers the mouse pointer over the link. PowerPoint also enables you to receive alerts about new links.

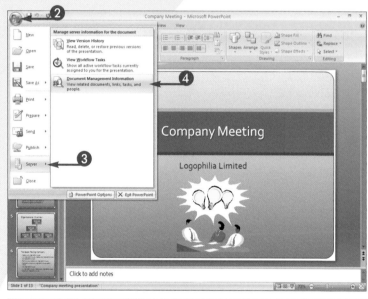

1 Open the presentation that is stored in the document workspace.

Note: If PowerPoint asks whether you want to get the latest version from the document workspace, click Get Updates.

2 Click the Office button.

3 Click Server.

4 Click Document Management Information.

Note: If you see the Connect dialog box, type your user name and password and click OK.

The Document Management task pane appears.

5 Click the Links button.

6 Click Add new link.

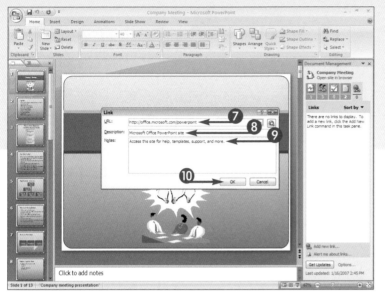

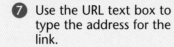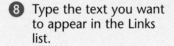

The Link dialog box appears.

7 Use the URL text box to type the address for the link.

8 Type the text you want to appear in the Links list.

9 Type the text that appears when you position the mouse pointer over the link.

10 Click OK.

● PowerPoint adds the link to the Links list.

TIPS

Did You Know?
You can also browse to the Web site you want to link to if you do not know its address. In Step **7** above, click the Browse button beside the URL text box; your browser opens. Browse to the Web page you want to link to, and then return to PowerPoint. The address is automatically inserted in the URL text box. Proceed with Step **8** to complete adding the link.

More Options!
You can choose to receive an e-mail alert when any of the links on the Document Management task pane change. On the Links tab of the Document Management task pane, click Alert me about links to sign up for alerts.

Chapter 10

Deliver and Distribute Your Presentation Effectively

You can deliver effective presentations regardless of whether your audience is live or your presentations are available for off-line or unattended use. You can create a custom show that displays only a subset of the slides in a presentation. You can hide slides so that they do not appear during presentation unless you specifically bring them up.

You can use Rehearse Timings to practice your presentation and determine how long it will take to present each slide. You can even program your presentation to replay after the last slide when you need to repeat a presentation.

If you have a Tablet PC, you can use your pen input device to draw on your Tablet PC screen and display that ink directly on your slides. You can create presentations for viewers to play in your absence by creating a kiosk presentation. Kiosk presentations play in Slide Show mode and advance automatically to the next slide. You can also present with multiple monitors and take advantage of PowerPoint's presenter view. You can even burn your presentation to a CD and make it available for use by viewers who do not have PowerPoint.

Top 100

CREATE A CUSTOM SHOW
instead of a new presentation

You can create a custom slide show to save time and reduce the need to update multiple versions of slide shows. Custom slide shows are collections of slides in a presentation that you can play together. For example, if you have a large presentation that outlines your company's products and services, you may want to create a custom show that displays only slides about new products or a show that presents slides only about your company and its services. When it is time to deliver your presentation, you can choose the custom show to play in Slide Show mode.

Without custom shows, you would probably have to create a different version of the presentation for each audience or for each use. This approach takes up more hard disk space and makes it difficult to perform updates because you have to find and then update each presentation. When you create custom shows, you keep all of the slides in the same presentation, which saves time and simplifies updating.

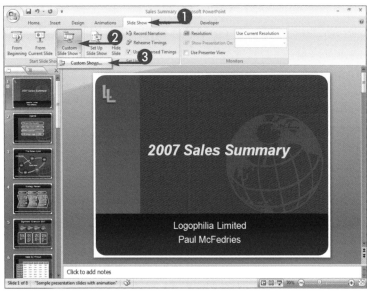

① Click the Slide Show tab.

② Click Custom Slide Show.

③ Click Custom Shows.

The Custom Shows dialog box appears.

④ Click New.

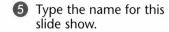

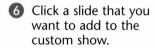

The Define Custom Show dialog box appears.

⑤ Type the name for this slide show.

⑥ Click a slide that you want to add to the custom show.

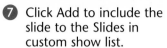

⑦ Click Add to include the slide to the Slides in custom show list.

⑧ Repeat Steps **6** and **7** until your list contains all the slides you want to include in the custom show.

⑨ Click OK.

The Define Custom Show dialog box closes, and the Custom Shows dialog box is again visible.

● PowerPoint adds the show to the Custom shows list.

⑩ Click Close.

PowerPoint saves your custom show.

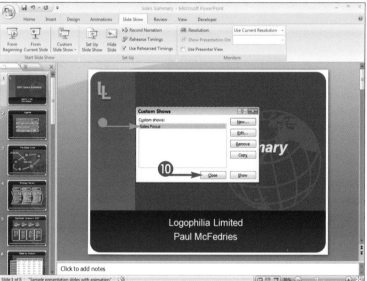

TIPS

Did You Know?

You can also create custom shows as a way to reorder slides for a given audience. For example, if presentation time is limited, you can create a custom show that presents your most important slides first in case you run out of time.

Test It!

To play a custom show, click Slide Show and then Custom Shows. In the Custom Shows dialog box, click the custom show you want to play, and then click Show.

Delete It!

You can easily delete custom shows. Follow Steps **1** to **3** above, and then click the show you want to delete in the Custom Shows dialog box. Click Remove and then click Close. The custom show is deleted.

DISPLAY HIDDEN SLIDES
during a presentation

You can include slides in your presentation that do not print in handouts or appear in presentations unless you specifically bring them up. These slides are called *hidden slides,* and they can be very useful when you have material that you may need to present, but you are not sure.

For example, if you are presenting a complex or detailed subject, you may be uncertain how well audience members will respond to the material. You may wonder whether they will have additional

questions or whether the basic material will be enough for them. In this case, you can include slides in your presentation that are ready for use, but only if you deliberately go to them during your presentation. Similarly, you can use hidden slides when you have a time limit and are not sure whether you can complete all slides during a given time period.

When you give your presentation, the hidden slides are omitted unless you use Go To Slide to advance to a hidden slide.

HIDE SLIDES

① Click the View tab.

② Click Slide Sorter.

The presentation appears in Slide Sorter view.

③ Click the Slide Show tab.

④ Click the slide you want to hide.

⑤ Click Hide Slide.

⑥ Repeat Steps **4** and **5** for all the slides you want to hide.

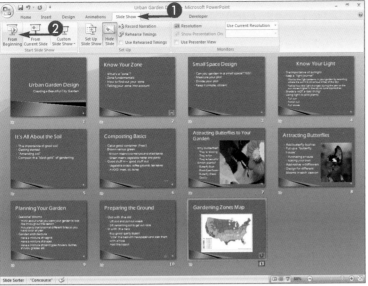

① Click the Slide Show
tab.

② Click From Beginning.

DIFFICULTY LEVEL

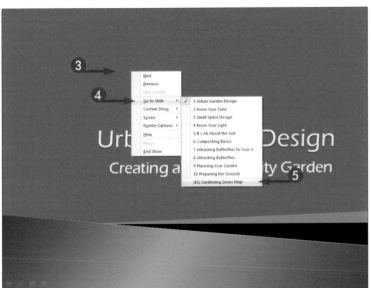

The presentation opens in Slide Show
mode.

③ Right-click the slide.

④ Click Go to Slide.

The list of slides appears.

⑤ Click the hidden slide you want to view.

The hidden slide opens.

TIPS

Attention!

Hidden slides appear in Slide Show mode with a line
through the slide number underneath each slide. The
Slide Sorter is the fastest way to tell which slides are
hidden.

Change It!

By default, hidden slides are not printed. If you want
the slide to print, click the Office button and then
Print. In the Print dialog box, click the Print hidden
slides check box (☐ changes to ☑).

Did You Know?

When you use Go to Slide during a presentation,
hidden slides are shown with the slide number in
parentheses. For example, a non-hidden slide might
appear as 2 Agenda, and a hidden slide might appear
as (2) Agenda.

Practice your presentation with
REHEARSE TIMINGS

You can practice your presentation and record the amount of time each slide needs when you use Rehearse Timings. For example, if you are preparing to give a presentation where your time is limited, you can practice delivering your presentation so that you know whether you are spending too much time on one slide or not enough on another. Instead of using a stopwatch to manually record the timings, PowerPoint can do the work for you.

When you use Rehearse Timings, PowerPoint displays your presentation in Slide Show mode, and the

Rehearsal toolbar appears. Every time you advance to the next slide, PowerPoint automatically records the time you spent on the previous slide. Timings appear beneath each slide in Slide Sorter view.

Rehearse Timings is also a good way to assign times to slides that you use in unattended presentations. For example, if you create a kiosk presentation, slides in the presentation advance using the timings set when you use Rehearse Timings.

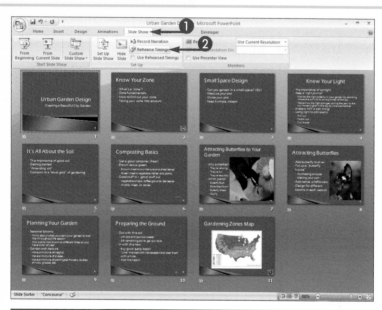

① Click the Slide Show tab.

② Click Rehearse Timings.

The slide show begins and the Rehearsal toolbar appears.

③ Go through the slide points and explanations exactly as you would during an actual presentation.

④ Click the Next icon to advance to the next slide.

⑤ Repeat Steps **3** and **4** for all of the slides in your presentation.

After the last slide in the presentation, the Microsoft Office PowerPoint dialog box appears, asking if you want to keep the slide timing for future use.

6 Click Yes.

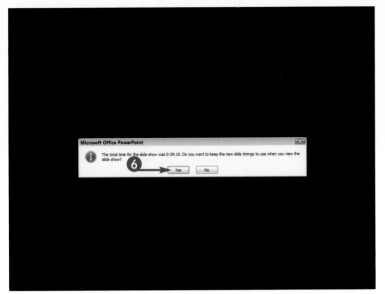

The presentation appears in Slide Sorter view with the slide timings noted under each slide.

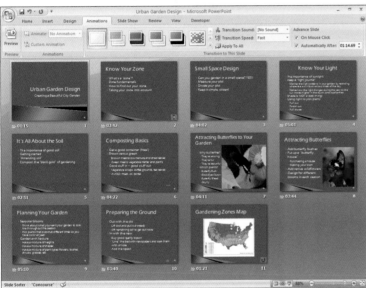

TIPS

Try This!

If you are interrupted while rehearsing a presentation, you can temporarily suspend the rehearsal. To do this, click the Pause button (⏸) on the Rehearsal toolbar. PowerPoint stops the timings. When you are ready to continue rehearsing, click the Pause button again to resume the timings.

Change It!

You can manually change slide timings for a slide. Click the slide for which you want to change the timing, and then click Animations. Click the Automatically After check box (◎ changes to ◉) and then use the associated text box or spin button to enter the number of seconds you want to use for the slide.

Repeat your presentation with
CONTINUOUS LOOPS

You can set up your presentation to replay continuously by moving from the last slide back to the first slide in your presentation. This option is available by using the Set Up Show dialog box to continually loop your presentation until you press the Esc key.

The ability to loop presentations is especially useful when you have to repeat a presentation without interruption between sessions. For example, if you have to deliver a presentation repeatedly in a booth at a trade show, looping the presentation saves time because you no longer have to stop and restart the presentation after every delivery.

Without the ability to continually loop the presentation, when you finish delivering your presentation in Slide Show mode, the presentation goes back to Normal view in PowerPoint, which you would not want the audience to see, especially when your presentation is being projected onto a large screen. Instead, when you continually loop the presentation, you can advance from the last slide to the first without interruption because the presentation stays in Slide Show mode the entire time.

① Click the Slide Show tab.

② Click Set Up Slide Show.

The Set Up Show dialog box appears.

③ Click the Loop continuously until 'Esc' check box (☐ changes to ☑).

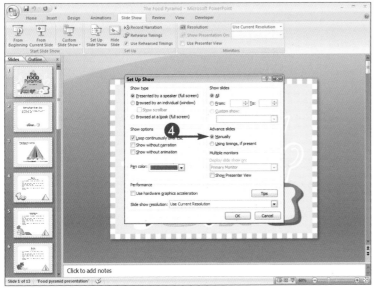

④ Click the Manually option (◯ changes to ⬤).

#94

DIFFICULTY LEVEL

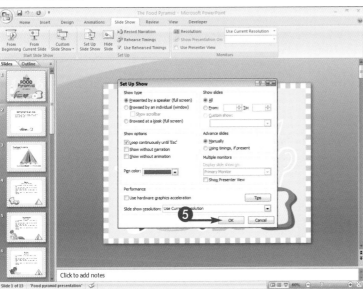

⑤ Click OK.

The slide show is set to repeat continuously until you press the Esc key.

TIPS

Did You Know?

You can use slide timings instead of manually advancing each slide. Follow the steps above, but in Step **4** click the Using timings, if present option (◯ changes to ⬤) instead of the Manually option (⬤ changes to ◯).

Did You Know?

You can create a presentation that loops only selected slides instead of all slides. Follow Steps **1** to **4** above. In the Show slides area, click the From option (◯ changes to ⬤). Use the spin buttons to click the slide number to start with and the slide number to end with, and then proceed with Step **5**.

ADD COMMENTS
during your presentations

If you have a Tablet PC computer, you can use your pen input device to add free-form notes and annotations to your slides while you give a presentation. The Tablet PC pen input device allows you to draw on your computer screen, and your drawings are enhanced with colorful lines that look like they are part of the slides.

When you view your presentation in Slide Show mode, you can tap the pen symbol with your pen input device to see the options available while

working with ink during your presentation. Options include selecting a pen type, which changes the width and shape of the displayed ink, and changing the color of the ink itself.

After ink is turned on while you are in Slide Show mode, you can draw freely on your computer screen, and those drawings are immediately visible to viewers. You can also change colors or pen type during your presentation.

① Click the Slide Show tab.

② Click From Beginning.

The presentation opens in Slide Show mode.

③ Display the first slide to which you want to add comments.

④ With your pen input device, tap the Pen icon.

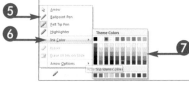

Who's Who

- President: Paul McFedries
- Treasurer: Karen Hammond
- IT: Brian Evans
- Personnel: Tessa Rubinstein
- Payroll: Pat Munson

⑤ →
⑥ →

⑦

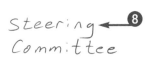

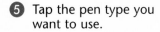
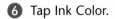

The content menu appears.

⑤ Tap the pen type you want to use.

⑥ Tap Ink Color.

⑦ In the palette that appears, tap the ink color that you want to use.

95

DIFFICULTY LEVEL

Who's Who

- President: Paul McFedries   } Steering ← **⑧**
- Treasurer: Karen Hammond   } Committee
- IT: Brian Evans
- Personnel: Tessa Rubinstein
- Payroll: Pat Munson

✳ Sales: Mike Redmond

⑧ Proceed with your presentation, using ink to annotate the slides as desired.

TIPS

More Options!
When you have finished delivering your presentation, you can save the ink with the slides or discard the ink on the slides.

Did You Know?
Ink that you save with your slides is visible to all viewers of your presentation, including those who do not use a Tablet PC. It also prints on your slides by default.

Try This!
You can choose the primary ink color for a presentation before you enter Slide Show mode. Click Slide Show and then Set Up Slide Show. In the Set Up Show dialog box, use the Pen Color list to click the color you want to use, and then click OK.

CREATE A KIOSK PRESENTATION
that runs unattended

You can create a presentation that runs when unattended. Kiosk presentations play full screen in Slide Show mode repeatedly until interrupted. Kiosk presentations are ideal when you want viewers to see your presentation but are not physically present to advance slides or restart the presentation when it is complete. For example, kiosk presentations are ideal for store windows and displays next to product merchandise.

Kiosk presentations rely on slide timings to determine when a slide should advance to the next one. Slide

timings are set by using Rehearse Timings, which enables you to rehearse your presentation and records the amount of time you spend on each slide (see Task #93). When your presentation plays, slides advance according to the times set when you rehearsed your presentation.

After slide timings are set, the slide show is set up to display the presentation at the maximum screen size available and to use the slide timings. When the presentation enters Slide Show mode, it continues to play until the Esc key is pressed.

① Rehearse the slide show timings, if you have not done so already.

Note: See Task #93 to learn how to use the Rehearse Timings feature.

② Click the Slide Show tab.

③ Click Set Up Slide Show.

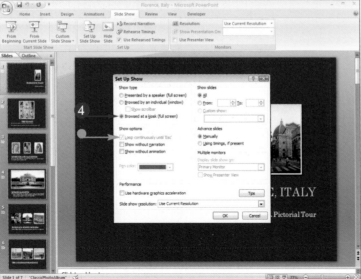

The Set Up Show dialog box appears.

④ Click the Browsed at a kiosk (full screen) option (◯ changes to ◉).

● PowerPoint automatically activates the Loop continuously until 'Esc' check box (☐ changes to ☑).

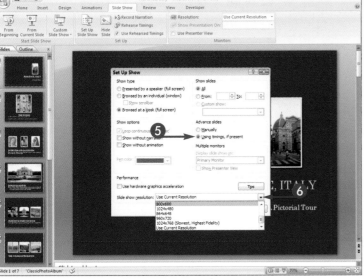

5 Click the Use timings, if present option (◎ changes to ⦿)

6 If the kiosk presentation uses a special monitor that supports a specific resolution, click here and select that resolution.

 # 96

DIFFICULTY LEVEL

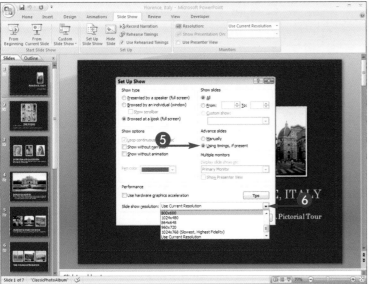

7 Click OK.

The next time you enter Slide Show mode, the presentation advances automatically using the timings you set and continually repeats after it is finished.

TIPS

Did You Know?

A kiosk presentation does not have a human presenter to generate or maintain audience interest. To help remedy this problem, note that kiosk presentations work well with multimedia content. For example, presentations with slide transitions, audio, video, and animations can be more attention-getting than plain presentations, and work well in kiosk mode.

More Options!

By default, kiosk presentations play the narration associated with a presentation (see Task #58). If you would prefer that PowerPoint not play the narration during the kiosk presentation, follow Steps **1** to **3**, click the Show without narration check box (☐ changes to ☑), and then continue with Step **4**.

WORK WITH MULTIPLE MONITORS
and Presenter View

You can configure PowerPoint to use two monitors for your presentation — one that only you see and one the audience sees. In the monitor that you see, you can perform some other action. The most common scenario is to use your monitor to display Presenter view and use its tools to make running a show easier. Presenter view shows a screen split into three sections: one for the current slide, another for the current slide's Notes page, and a third that shows thumbnail images of the presentation's slides — you can use

these thumbnails to look ahead in the presentation and to quickly navigate to a specific slide. The Presenter view also shows the slide show navigation tools.

Before you can use Presenter View, you need to attach a second monitor to your computer, or attach an external monitor to your notebook computer. You then configure that monitor in Windows (see the Tip on the next page). You can then set up the slide show to use the multiple monitors.

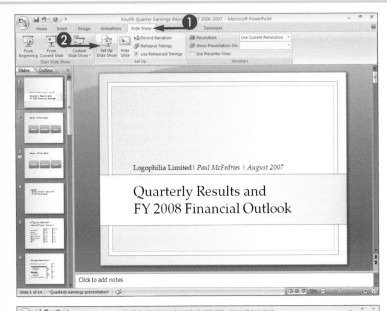

SET UP MULTIPLE MONITORS
① Click the Slide Show tab.

② Click Set Up Slide Show.

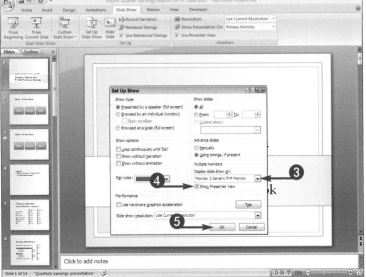

The Set Up Show dialog box appears.

③ Click here and select the monitor on which you want to show the presentation.

④ Click the Show Presenter View check box (☐ changes to ✓).

⑤ Click OK.

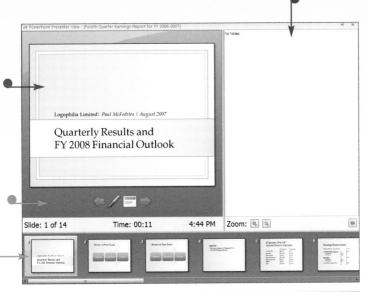

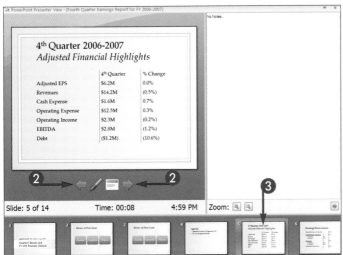

1 Press F5.

The slide show begins playing.

● The presenter's monitor (the monitor that you did *not* select in Step 4 of "Set Up Multiple Monitors" on the opposite page) shows the Presenter view, with tools for navigating in and delivering the presentation.

● The current slide appears.

● The Notes page for the current slide appears.

● Thumbnails for each slide appear.

2 Click an arrow button to move forward and backwards through the slides.

Note: The other two slide show control buttons that appear under the current slide work as in a normal slide show, enabling you to work with annotation settings and navigate the show.

3 Click a slide thumbnail in the pane at the bottom to jump to that slide.

4 Press Esc at any time to end the presentation.

DIFFICULTY LEVEL

97

TIPS

Attention!

Before you can use a second monitor in PowerPoint, you need to configure the extra monitor in Windows. In Windows Vista, click Start, click Control Panel, and then under Appearance and Personalization, click Adjust screen resolution. Click the 2 icon, click Extend the desktop onto this monitor (☐ changes to ☑), and then click OK.

More Options!

A computer that has a video adapter with a graphics coprocessor can help speed up the display on your monitor. If you have such hardware in your computer, click the Slide Show tab, then click Set Up Slide Show to display the Set Up Show dialog box. Click the Use hardware graphics acceleration check box (☐ changes to ☑), and then click OK.

START AUTOMATICALLY

You can run a slide show quickly by saving the presentation as a PowerPoint Show file that runs automatically when you double-click it.

Ordinarily, PowerPoint 2007 stores presentations using the default PowerPoint Presentation format, which uses the .pptx file extension. Double-clicking such a file in Windows Explorer opens the presentation in the PowerPoint program window. From there, you use the PowerPoint Ribbon commands or keyboard shortcuts to launch the slide show.

However, you can save a few steps by creating a file that bypasses the PowerPoint window and goes straight to the slide show. You do this by saving a presentation using the PowerPoint Show (PPS) format, which uses the .ppsx file extension. Double-clicking a PPS file in Windows Explorer launches the slide show right away without having to first negotiate the PowerPoint window. This is also a safe way to distribute a presentation because it means the other users can only view the slide show; they cannot open the presentation in PowerPoint and make changes to it.

SAVE THE POWERPOINT SHOW FILE

① Click the Office button.

② Click the Save As arrow.

③ Click PowerPoint Show.

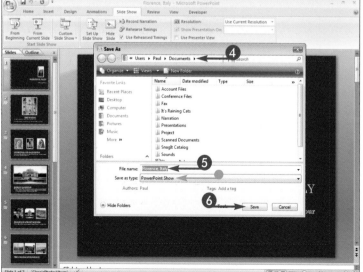

The Save As dialog box appears.

● The PowerPoint Show format is automatically selected in the Save as type list.

④ Select the folder in which you want to save the file.

⑤ Edit the File name, if desired.

⑥ Click Save.

PowerPoint saves the file.

① Use Windows Explorer to open the folder that contains the PowerPoint Show file.

② Click the PowerPoint Show file.

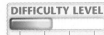

● To confirm you have the correct file, look for Microsoft Office PowerPoint Slide Show in the Details pane.

③ Double-click the PowerPoint Show file.

The file's slide show begins automatically.

FLORENCE, ITALY

A Pictorial Tour

TIPS

Try This!

If the users that you want to view the PowerPoint Show file have earlier versions of PowerPoint (2003, XP, 2000, or 97), create a PowerPoint Show file for those earlier versions. Click Office and then click Save As to open the Save As dialog box. In the Save as type list, click PowerPoint 97-2003 Show, and then click Save.

More Options!

If you want to prevent other people from making changes to your presentation, you can apply a password to the file. Click Office and then click Save As to open the Save As dialog box. Click Tools, click General Options, type a password in the Password to modify text box, and then click OK. Confirm the password and then click OK.

Distribute your presentation with the
POWERPOINT VIEWER

You can make your presentation available to viewers even if they are not PowerPoint users by including the PowerPoint Viewer 2007 program with your presentation. The PowerPoint Viewer 2007 is available free from the Microsoft Download Center.

For example, if you create a presentation about your products and want to distribute that presentation to your customers, you may be concerned about what to do if they do not have PowerPoint 2007. To ensure that they can view your presentation, even if it is password-protected, you can send them the PowerPoint

Viewer 2007 along with your presentation. Recipients of your presentation then run the PowerPoint Viewer 2007, open your presentation, and it plays.

You can download the PowerPoint Viewer 2007 to your computer using the Microsoft Download Center. You can then post the file on a shared network for others to access. For users not on your network, you cannot send the PowerPoint Viewer 2007 program via e-mail because it is too large. Either send them the Microsoft download link or publish the presentation to a PDF or XPS file (see Task #73).

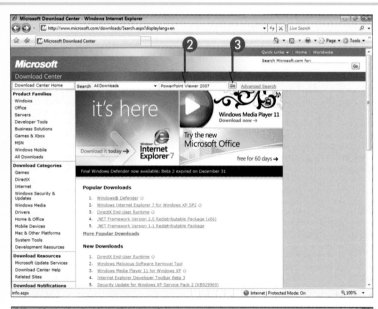

① In your Web browser, go to www.microsoft.com/downloads.

② In the Search text box, type **PowerPoint Viewer 2007**.

③ Click Go.

The Microsoft Download Center displays the search results.

④ Click the PowerPoint Viewer 2007 link.

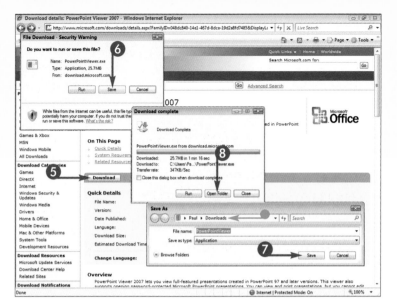

The PowerPoint Viewer 2007 download page appears.

5 Click Download.

6 Click Save.

● Your user profile's Downloads folder is automatically selected.

7 Click Save.

8 When the download is complete, click Open Folder.

DIFFICULTY LEVEL

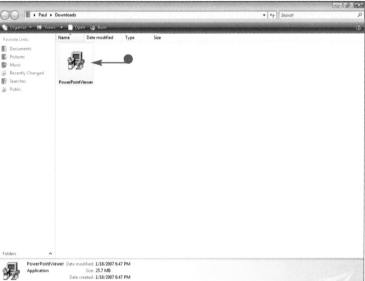

● The Download folder appears and you see the PowerPointViewer file.

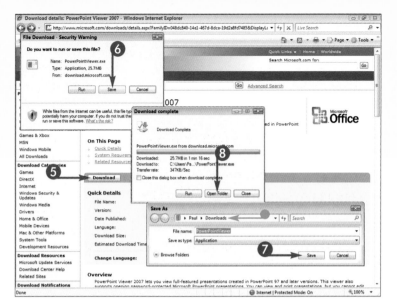

TIPS

Important!

PowerPoint Viewer 2007 is designed for playing back presentations that have been created with PowerPoint 97 or later. Users of PowerPoint Viewer 2007 can view presentations, but they cannot edit them.

Caution!

Unlike previous versions of PowerPoint Viewer, the latest version is quite large — nearly 26MB. Do not distribute this file to users who have a slow Internet connection or a limit on the size of e-mail attachments.

Caution!

You cannot view presentations that use Information Rights Management or embedded macros, programs, or linked objects in PowerPoint Viewer 2007. Otherwise, even multimedia effects, transitions, and more work in PowerPoint Viewer 2007.

BURN A PRESENTATION CD
for a wider distribution

You can make your presentation available to a larger audience when you burn it to a CD and then distribute it. The Package for CD command makes it easy and automatic to publish and then burn all of the files that are needed directly onto a CD.

Without Package for CD, you would need to create a new directory, save the PowerPoint Viewer 2007 (see Task #99) to that directory, save your presentation there, and then have a developer create all of the files necessary to make the CD play automatically when it

is inserted into the recipient's CD drive. After that work is complete, you must burn the files to a CD.

PowerPoint 2007 simplifies the process. You assign a name to the CD, and then instruct PowerPoint to copy the files to the CD. PowerPoint communicates with your computer's CD burner to copy all of the necessary files along with your presentation onto the CD. When the recipient inserts the CD into his or her CD drive, it automatically opens the PowerPoint Viewer 2007 and plays the presentation.

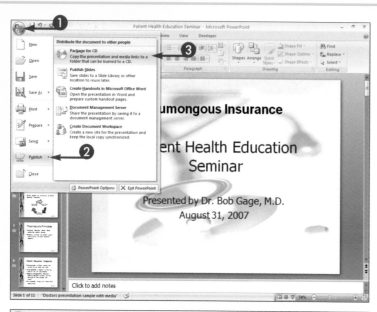

① Click the Office button.

② Click Publish.

③ Click Package for CD.

PowerPoint lets you know that it will convert your files to the PowerPoint 97-2003 format.

④ Click OK.

The Package for CD dialog box appears.

⑤ Type the name of the CD.

⑥ Insert a recordable CD into your CD burner.

⑦ Click Copy to CD.

⑧ Click Yes.

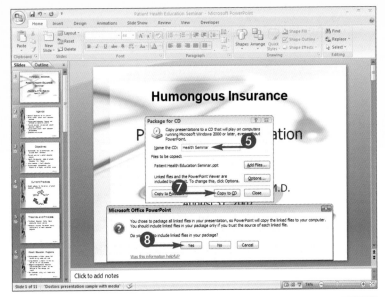

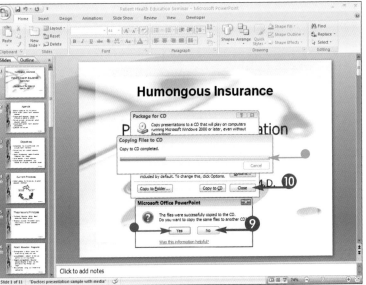

● The Copying Files to CD dialog box appears, displaying a progress indicator for the status of the copy process. When the process completes, the Microsoft Office PowerPoint dialog box appears.

⑨ Click No.

● If you want to create duplicate copies of the CD, insert a new recordable CD and then click Yes, instead.

⑩ Click Close.

All the files you need for distributing the presentation are on the CD.

TIPS

More Options!
To control the CD burning process yourself, PowerPoint can copy all the necessary files to a folder instead of the CD. Follow Steps **1** to **5** above, and then click Copy to Folder in the Package for CD dialog box.

Did You Know?
In Step **5**, the name you assign to the CD is the name that appears next to the recipient's CD drive letter in Windows Explorer. Therefore, you should name your CD carefully.

Try This!
You can add additional files to the CD. For example, for a presentation about new products, you might want to include a product brochure or price list on the CD. Follow Steps **1** to **5** above, and then click Add Files in the Package for CD dialog box.

Chapter 10: Deliver and Distribute Your Presentation Effectively   221

Index

Symbols and Numbers

Index

Index

Index

...all designed for visual learners—just like you!

Master VISUALLY®

Step up to intermediate-to-advanced technical knowledge. Two-color interior.

- 3dsMax
- Creating Web Pages
- Dreamweaver and Flash
- Excel VBA Programming
- iPod and iTunes
- Mac OS
- Optimizing PC Performance
- Photoshop Elements
- QuickBooks
- Quicken
- Windows
- Windows Mobile
- Windows Server

Visual Blueprint™

Where to go for professional-level programming instruction. Two-color interior.

- Ajax
- Excel Data Analysis
- Excel Pivot Tables
- Excel Programming
- HTML
- JavaScript
- Mambo
- PHP & MySQL
- Visual Basic

Visual Encyclopedia™

Your A to Z reference of tools and techniques. Full color.

- Dreamweaver
- Excel
- Photoshop
- Windows

Visual Quick Tips™

Shortcuts, tricks, and techniques for getting more done in less time. Full color.

- Digital Photography
- Excel
- MySpace
- Office
- PowerPoint
- Windows
- Wireless Networking

...all designed for visual learners—just like you!

Master VISUALLY®

Step up to intermediate-to-advanced technical knowledge. Two-color interior.

- 3dsMax
- Creating Web Pages
- Dreamweaver and Flash
- Excel VBA Programming
- iPod and iTunes
- Mac OS
- Optimizing PC Performance
- Photoshop Elements
- QuickBooks
- Quicken
- Windows
- Windows Mobile
- Windows Server

Visual Blueprint™

Where to go for professional-level programming instruction. Two-color interior.

- Ajax
- Excel Data Analysis
- Excel Pivot Tables
- Excel Programming
- HTML
- JavaScript
- Mambo
- PHP & MySQL
- Visual Basic

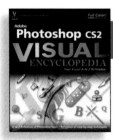

Visual Encyclopedia™

Your A to Z reference of tools and techniques. Full color.

- Dreamweaver
- Excel
- Photoshop
- Windows

Visual Quick Tips™

Shortcuts, tricks, and techniques for getting more done in less time. Full color.

- Digital Photography
- Excel
- MySpace
- Office
- PowerPoint
- Windows
- Wireless Networking

For a complete listing of Visual books, go to wiley.com/go/visual

Visual®
An Imprint of ⓌW
Now you know